What people are saying about the recipes in *Delicious Gluten-Free Wheat-Free Breads*

"I can't tell you how much I enjoyed tasting a variety of breads after so many years of abstinence–or the cardboard gluten-free breads that are commercially available. These recipes re-open the door to delicious baked goods once again. The Reuben Bread is absolutely extraordinary!

My top 10 breads from this book are:

1. Reuben	*2. Blue Cornmeal*
3. Broccoli Cheese	*4. Sundried Tomato*
5. Zucchini Blueberry	*6. Fig and Almond*
7. Chicken and Peppers	*8. Date, Cumin and Coriander*
9. Date Nut	*10. Pineapple Macadamia*
11. Gruyere	*12. Mustard Rye*

Okay, I couldn't limit it to 10. These were all just excellent!

—Kathy Bowers

"I never really liked bread as a kid so I didn't really care when the doctor told me at 48 years old that I had celiac and couldn't have bread anymore. After taste testing all of these recipes, I have suddenly discovered a world of wonderful breads."

—Linda Taroli

"These breads made me excited about eating bread again! I didn't know how much I missed eating sandwiches until I tasted these breads! Each and every bread is perfect for a variety of toppings and uses. I loved these breads, even the ones I didn't think I would."

—Tanya Chakravarty

"I had the honor to taste different recipes from Delicious Gluten-Free Wheat-Free Breads. *I am not gluten-free, but the texture of the breads was moist and the flavors were inviting. I would not have known they were gluten-free."*

—Shanna Murphree

"Delicious Gluten-Free Wheat-Free Breads *is a blessing in a book."*

—Vicki Bizallion

"The recipes and instructions in Delicious Gluten-Free Wheat- Free Breads *are easy to follow. I particularly like the hints and tips and the different baking methods."*

—Doug Magee

"Delicious Gluten-Free Wheat-Free Breads *is a great example of a well written cookbook. It is inventive and creative with a personal style that reaches out to a wide variety of tastes. Well done!"*

—Charlie Nygaard

"I liked how easy all of the recipes were to understand."

—Laurie Ann Pepin

Delicious

Gluten-Free
Wheat-Free

Breads

Easy to Make Breads
Everyone will Love to Eat
For the Bread Machine—Or Oven

Includes the new *No-Knead—No-Rise* Method
suitable for most breads

LynnRae Ries, author
Bruce Gross, co-author
Loni Frankland-Twomey, illustrator

Foreword by Michelle Pietzak, M.D.

Celiac Disease, Gluten Intolerance, Dermatitis Herpetiformis Information
by Michelle Pietzak, M.D., Director, Center for Celiac Research—West

Food Allergy information from The Food Allergy & Anaphylaxis Network

Interactive website information and updates relating to this book
and author at www.lynnrae.com

Delicious Gluten-Free Wheat-Free Breads
Easy to Make Breads Everyone will Love to Eat for the Bread Machine–or Oven

First edition

Published by What? No What? Publishing Company
4757 East Greenway Road, Suite 103 - #91
Phoenix, Arizona 85032
800-777-1242 E-mail: whatnowheat@whatnowheat.com

Visit our website at www.whatnowheat.com for more information on this series and other publications.

Visit the author's website at www.lynnrae.com for more information on this book and updates as well as other publications.

Interior design by Lisa Liddy, The Printed Page, www.theprintedpage.com
Cover design by LynnRae Ries and Lisa Liddy, The Printed Page
Illustrations by Loni Frankland-Twomey, 925-606-6753

Ries, LynnRae
Delicious Gluten-Free Wheat-Free Breads. Easy to make
Breads Everyone will Love to Eat for the Bread Machine–or Oven
By LynnRae Ries 1st ed.
Includes Index
ISBN 0-9724154-1-6
LCCN 2002115557
1. Cookbooks 2. Special Diets 3. Celiac Disease 4. Gluten Intolerance
5. Wheat free diet

Many people experiment with different grains and baking techniques for a variety of reasons. This book is not intended to be a complete source for information on all grains or techniques available. It is also not intended to take the place of your health care professional. Do not start a totally gluten-free or wheat-free diet without seeking medical assistance. The publisher and author are not responsible for any errors, omissions or misstatements that may exist within this publication. This publication is not to be construed as the whole or entire information on the subject of baking, ingredients, processes or any of the medical conditions or personal choices associated with a gluten-free or wheat-free diet.

I remember my Grandmother as a kind, generous and loving Swedish woman. One of the many ways she shared and showed her love was by baking.

Grandma would rise early and spend all day baking breads, cinnamon rolls, caramel rolls, cookies, and pies. She never measured the ingredients; her style was simply to toss in a handful of this and a dash of that.

Many loaves of bread taught Grandma to know by look, by touch, and by smell, when the dough mixture was ready. She had a great approach to baking—said it was a little bit like life—the results of some breads (days) are better than others.

We all watched in awe as Grandma would create her baking magic. She would sprinkle flour on the kitchen table and knead the dough until it was silky, then gave it a pat, place it in her favorite bread bowl and toss one of her treasured potato sack cloths over the top. We would all play Parcheesi on a home-made board or a friendly game of cards while we waited for the dough to balloon up to twice its size.

When the time came to put the bread into the oven, we started clearing the table in anticipation. It was like Heaven when Grandma pulled the bread from the oven an hour later. We would butter it when it was still hot, and sometimes slathered home-made apple butter over a slice or two.

Later in the day we would tuck a piece of cheddar cheese between two slices of bread or make a quick sandwich with a thick layer of peanut butter. We knew homemade bread was best on the day it was made, so we devoured as much as we could before it became even one day older.

Grandma's baking was always the star attraction. It was one of the special things that brought our family together in a spirit of joy.

Her baking and sharing the breads gave a deeper meaning to our lives—the love and thoughtfulness she put into the breads was something we all shared, something we all appreciated and something we all took home.

Dedication

This book is dedicated to those who made these memories possible,
my aunts, uncles, cousins, father, grandfather, sisters, and especially

To my Mother and Grandmother

A wish for you

May the breads created
through the recipes and methods
in this book bring you much happiness
and fond memories

—LynnRae

Contents

Foreword

"LynnRae Ries' book, *Delicious Gluten-Free Wheat-Free Breads,* is a welcome addition for people living a gluten-free or wheat-free life, whether it is due to celiac disease, gluten intolerance or a wheat allergy.

By combining the ease of the bread machine with a variety of baking methods, LynnRae, and her team of Testers and Tasters, responds to the need of being able to easily add bread back into the life of those who cannot eat wheat, rye or barley.

The interaction with the coordinating website, along with the option to personalize the recipes to match personal tastes, for convenience or to expand upon ones own creativity, adds even greater dimension to her book.

There is no doubt that LynnRae's book is an important addition to the gluten-free and wheat-free life, whether being used for celiac disease, gluten intolerance or wheat allergy.

Michelle Pietzak, M.D.
Assistant Professor of Clinical Pediatrics
University of Southern California Keck School of Medicine
Director, Center for Celiac Research—West

About This Book

Delicious Gluten-Free Wheat-Free Breads is ideal for those who want to venture into baking with new and different flours and techniques. It is also for people on a wheat-free or gluten-free diet due to a medical diagnosis such as celiac disease, gluten intolerance, food allergy, or at a doctor's suggestion.

Since I was diagnosed with celiac disease in 1999, this book grew out of the need to learn how to create breads that were tasty and easy to make. My first attempts at baking with gluten-free flours in the oven were disheartening. The breads would not rise, or they rose and fell. Sometimes they did not get done enough in the center, or they crumbled and fell apart, plus a multitude of other fiascos. Yet I was determined to learn how to bake bread the gluten-free way.

It was not bread itself that I missed.

- It was the convenience of being able to make a quick sandwich.
- It was the pleasure of having a hamburger in a bun at a barbeque with everyone else.
- It was the freedom of not being restricted to only the few gluten-free types of bread in the frozen section of the grocery store—as grateful as I was, and am, that they are available.

I knew that living a gluten-free life would be much easier if I could make my own bread, and then share the joy with others, either by baking for them, or by helping them learn to bake for themselves.

Initially I practiced baking bread by myself. Vern and I then traveled to take cooking and baking classes from gluten-free cookbook authors and famous instructors, such as Bette Hagman, Carol Fenster, Jessica Hale and Yvonne Gifford of Glutenfreeda, Jane Butel and many others.

But I truly did not find a style of baking that worked for me until I tried the bread machine. Up until that time, I was certain yeast and I were mortal enemies.

The bread machine made all the difference in the world. It allowed me to bake as my Grandma did, with a freer hand rather than being so worried about exact measurements or ingredients.

The bread machine also made it so the breads were thoroughly mixed, doubled in size, baked through and tasted wonderful.

When I used the bread machine as a mixer and "safe place" for the dough to rise, I was also able to duplicate this bread making success in the oven.

Excited over these achievements, I started baking for other people who were gluten intolerant. Providing fresh bread, as well as other baked goods, quickly grew into a special order gluten-free baking service.

For almost three years I perfected recipes, added to my baking repertoire and shared the joy of freshly made delicious gluten-free baked items with others.

When I decided to write *Delicious Gluten-Free Wheat-Free Breads,* I was overwhelmed by the number of generous people who extended their hearts and hands to participate and help.

This book became a special project that brought together bread recipe Testers and bread Tasters for the purpose of learning and sharing the techniques and tastes that worked for us, and will for you.

Like at Grandma's house, it was a coming together in a spirit of joy. It was something we all shared and something we all enjoyed.

The recipes and techniques in this book are from our hearts to your home.

—LynnRae Ries

Getting Started

Whether you are baking gluten-free or wheat-free as a chosen personal adventure or due to a medical condition or allergy, the first important thing to do is to **determine which products are wheat gluten-free or wheat-free**.

Luckily, there are many sources available to help you.

- National support organizations
- Conferences
- Books, magazines and newsletters
- Gluten-free and wheat-free product manufacturers

Many of these sources are listed in the back of this book.

If choosing totally gluten-free or wheat-free products is due to a medical concern, you will need to read labels on every item you purchase and for every ingredient listed in a recipe. If you do not understand the label or any of the words, it will be necessary for you to either verify gluten-free ingredients with the manufacturer, check with a national support organization, or do without and find a substitute.

Once you have determined your products are gluten-free, you can **relax and allow yourself time to learn and enjoy what you are doing**.

You may be someone who is successful with your first loaf of bread—or you may not get the "hang of it" until the fourth loaf. Gluten-free bread is no different from a wheat bread in that category. The following thoughts may help you.

- The methods used in this book will show you it is possible to be successful in baking bread like our Grandmothers did—with a freer hand rather than being so worried about precise measurements or identical ingredients.
- Home baking is not an exact science. Some baking days just turn out better than others.
- Weather, humidity, geographical area can all affect the look or texture of the bread.
- Sources of flours can make a difference. The age of the flour, how long it has been in storage, when it was milled plus a number of other variables can make a difference in the end result.
- Gluten-free breads are not wheat breads. They will never be identical to wheat breads—they are simply not the same ingredients—but who said wheat breads are the ideal?

There are many important reasons for baking:

- It is a form of self expression—that is why we included an area to personalize each recipe.
- It can be soothing to the soul, especially when feeling stressed, that is why we included breads that reflect comfort and tradition, as well as those with character and interest.
- It is a learning and expanding process—that is why there is an interactive website as a companion to this book.

- Breads do not always stand alone—that is why we included over 50 recipes that go beyond breads, into toppings, sauces, spreads, meals, icings, and more.

Everyone is different, and so are the breads:

- It is interesting how two people will taste the very same thing—differently. When you bake bread that is perfect for your tastes, look at the ingredients to determine what you liked the most.
- If you encounter a recipe you do not care for, consider how you may personalize it to suit your tastes.
- Likewise, bread texture is interpreted differently by many people. Some like super moist bread, while others want it drier. Some people like a denser bread, others want it airy and light. And to some people determining if they like the "crumb" or "texture" of the bread is a moot point. They simply want an edible, enjoyable piece of bread.
- There are many reasons for enjoying bread. Dessert, sandwiches, as a meal, snacking, for breakfast, or as a component of something else, like stuffing or a bread pudding. Think about the purpose of the bread you are making. Is it for a sandwich? Perhaps you want it on the moist side. Is it as an appetizer? You may want it drier so it will hold up to the toppings.

Consider the different measuring styles and baking methods.

- How you measure your flours or starches into a measuring cup will be different from your neighbor, your best friend or your mother. Scoop, sprinkle, dust, sift, fluff, tap, mix are all words that may define how someone measures their flour. There is no right way—just the way that works for you.
- Worn out measuring cups that cause you to guess, different sized bread machine pans, dark oven bread pans versus light bread pans, they all can make a difference in your end result.
- Each baking method described in *Delicious Gluten-Free Wheat-Free Breads* makes a little different loaf of bread. The Two Step Method (Dough-Bake Cycles) is usually a little lighter than the One Step Method (Basic Cycle), and the No-Knead No-Rise Method may be a little "finer, moister or denser" than the other methods. But all the results are still contingent on how you measure your flours, handle your liquids, or interpret the baked bread from your own perspective.
- Each bread machine or oven will bake a little differently and produce a slightly different loaf of bread, either because of its size, or shape or the positioning of the heating elements.

Think of gluten-free bread baking as an adventure.

- Be consistent in your measuring. If you "scoop," always scoop. If you sift, always sift.
- Use the same pans, utensils, measuring cups and measuring spoons each time.
- Be aware of the variety of variables that may require adjustments to the recipe, such as the weather. Be positive. You will learn how to make adaptations so the end result is a beautiful loaf of bread.
- Learn the water ratio you need in order to make the best tasting bread—to you—and to those you love. That is why you will see a plus and minus after the water or liquid measurement in the recipes. A tablespoon or two less, or a tablespoon or two more can make a considerable difference in your bread. Further information on this subject is in the "Bread Machine Methods" section on page 125.

Suggestions for baking your first loaf of bread:

- Read your bread machine instructions carefully.
- Review the different baking methods in this book and determine which method you are going to use.
- Read your chosen recipe completely.
- Verify all ingredients you are using are wheat-gluten-free.
- Consider any other food allergies or intolerances you may have and plan accordingly for substitutions.
- Organize the ingredients in the order you will be putting them into the machine to avoid omissions or duplications.
- Have all of your ingredients at room temperature (if possible).
- Use the same measuring utensils for consistency. Store them in your bread machine if possible.

Now fire up your engines—your bread machines that is, and don't wait another minute before you start baking gluten-free bread. What? No bread machine yet? Then bake them in your oven.

How to Read Our Recipes

Every recipe is unique. It is like a thumbprint of the designer. As you use a recipe, modify it, adjust it or dissect it into a totally different recipe, it will become **your** thumbprint. The following bits of information are to help you learn how we designed our recipes so you may enjoy them as is, or personalize them enough to make them your own.

Our Recipe Writing Style

Each recipe is presented with a sense of continuity and conciseness, making it easier for you to learn the ingredients of the basic recipes by heart.

For instance, we could have written one recipe with 1½ teaspoons of salt and the next recipe with 1 teaspoons of salt. Instead, we chose to enhance your baking pleasure by avoiding tedious measurements that make very little difference in the end result. This will speed your assembly of ingredients, allow you to learn the recipe faster and give you ample opportunity to tailor ingredients to your particular needs.

We also chose to keep the core of each recipe to a minimum number of items. Each recipe focuses on the combination of quality ingredients that provide an interesting and delicious recipe suitable for the whole family, a wide variety of tastes and special occasions.

Wet Ingredients:

Eggs and substitutes

All of the recipes in this book use eggs as part of the binder, for leavening and to add moisture. You may also use an egg substitute. Total egg combination should equal ¾ cup.

- 1 whole egg plus enough egg whites to equal ¾ cup
- 2 whole eggs plus enough egg whites to equal ¾ cup
- 3 whole eggs plus enough egg whites to equal ¾ cup
- Liquid egg substitute to equal ¾ cup
- Powdered egg replacer. One Tester used 4½ teaspoons of powdered egg replacer and added it to ¾ cup of water or juice used in the recipe and waited until it was well dissolved before adding to the wet ingredients. The breads all rose nicely.

Egg whites alone are sold in pourable containers in the refrigerated section of the grocery store usually with the eggs. Using an egg replacer may result in a loaf that does not rise as high. The Testers used a combination of whole eggs and egg whites for the recipes in this book.

Your Key to Success—Liquid/Flour Ratio

The recipes all show a liquid amount with the phrase "plus or minus." Learning the "plus or minus" of the liquid ratio to the flours is key to successful bread baking.

Start with the amount of water suggested in the recipe. If the dough needs more water, add it one tablespoon at a time during the mix/knead cycle of your bread machine. Make a note of it in your recipe book. Allow a minute for the dough to absorb the water/liquid before adding another Tablespoon.

How will you know if the dough needs more water? The dough will be in a ball and may look dry. You want the dough to naturally spread to the sides of the pan and have a somewhat silky, smooth, batter-type appearance. Many Testers were able to see the lines of the paddle going around on top of the dough. Other Testers determined the dough had enough water when a small cap covered the paddle and the rest of the dough was smooth.

Why the difference in the liquid? The amount of water needed depends on the flours, the weather, the baker's techniques and the geographical location. Once you have made a couple of breads you will learn whether the recipe needs more or less liquid.

Liquid

Other ingredients may be used for your liquid; juices, sauces, potato water (tends to help the bread rise), colas, un-colas, milk or gluten-free milk substitutes. Most Testers used bottled water or potato water. One Tester used tap water with excellent results. If you use a liquid other than what is called for in the recipe, the substitute measurement may not be necessarily in direct proportion. All liquids should be at room temperature.

Oil

Specific oils or butter have been mentioned where we determined it made a difference in the recipe. There are many oils on the market; canola oil, vegetable oil, olive oil, nut oils, flavored oils, or seed oils. You may substitute the oil (not necessarily in direct proportion) with yogurt, sour cream, applesauce, mayonnaise, tofu, or baby food prune puree.

Vinegar

Vinegars add acidity to the bread mixture. Specific vinegars have been mentioned where we determined they made a difference in the recipe. For convenience, cider vinegar or plain rice vinegar could be used for all the recipes. Malt vinegar is not wheat- gluten-free as of the writing of this book. Lemon juice can be used as an emergency substitute for vinegar.

Dry Ingredients:

Each recipe calls for a specific mix of flours. We found these flours and starches to be the best mix for each particular recipe. During testing, starches were used interchangeably, with equally good results. We also made many of these recipes using ¼ cup or ½ flour substitutions and they all worked equally well.

Some of the recipes were tested using ready-made flour mixes. The bread had a different taste from the proven and taste-tested one in the recipe, but when made in the bread machine, they rose, baked through and were enjoyable.

We have provided space for personalizing your recipe whether it's for the convenience of your own mix, or a prepackaged flour mix, because of substitution due to an allergy, or for the pure joy of developing your own creation.

Flours and Starches

The following is a brief description of the dry goods used in this book. There are many other gluten-free flours, starches and dry goods available. Contact companies from the "Resource" section of this book to request their catalog and verify wheat gluten-free status of items.

Amaranth bran flour is a combination of amaranth flour and amaranth bran that is lightly toasted to create a sweet toasty, nutty flavor.

Amaranth flour is produced from tiny grain-like tan seeds. It is high in protein and contains Vitamin A and C.

Brown rice flour is ground from nutty tasting brown rice. It is higher in fiber, vitamins and minerals than white rice flour.

Buckwheat flour is high in fiber, iron and B vitamins. It is related to rhubarb, not wheat.

Corn flour is milled from corn.

Cornstarch is a refined starch from corn.

Garbanzo bean flour is ground garbanzo beans, also known as chickpeas.

Garfava bean flour is a combination of bean flours, namely the garbanzo bean and fava bean.

Millet flour has a more nearly complete protein than other common grains. It comes from a round seed that grows in tropical climates.

Potato flour is not used in any of the recipes in this book. It is not the same as Potato Starch.

Potato starch is a fine white starch made from potatoes.

Sweet potato starch is made from sweet potatoes.

Tapioca starch flour is a fine white starch made from the cassava plant. You may see packages labeled as Tapioca Flour. It is usually the same as Tapioca starch flour.

Quinoa flour is ground quinoa seeds. It creates a delicate, cake-like crumb and has a pleasant, nutty taste.

Sorghum flour adds hearty protein and flavor. It is grey in color and adds moisture to baked goods.

Soy flour is milled from soybeans and has a slightly nutty taste with a strong flavor.

Sweet rice flour is ground from glutinous rice–meaning "sticky" rice. It is not interchangeable with most flours.

White rice flour is milled from polished rice. Look for the finest texture possible.

Other Dry Ingredients:

Salt enhances the flavor of the recipe. A single teaspoon was used in all these recipes. Sea salt, kosher salt and table salt were all used with no discernable difference in bread results.

Dry Milk Powder is usually skim milk that has been dried using a low temperature drying process. It adds flavor, color, nutrients and keeping qualities to the bread. It also enhances the color. It may be omitted for those who are lactose intolerant.

Sugar is a necessary part of bread recipes both for taste and to assist the yeast to rise. We used light molasses, robust molasses, light brown sugar, dark brown sugar, granulated sugar, brown rice syrup, maple syrup, corn syrup and honey as our sugars.

Meals

- **Cornmeal** is ground from corn.
- **Flaxseed meal** is finely ground flax seeds.

- **Nut meals, also known as nut flours**. Almost any nut can be finely ground into a meal or flour with a food processor. Almond meal, Hazelnut meal and Macadamia meal are used in this book.

Rye Flavor Powder is available from Authentic Foods.

Caramel Color is a powder produced from sweeteners. It gives baked products a darker color.

Dough Enhancer is a combination of yeast, ascorbic acid and other ingredients that combine together to improve the dough and give it longer shelf life. Not all dough enhancers are wheat gluten-free. One Tester used dough enhancer in all the breads. Other Testers did not use it and still achieved great results.

Xanthan Gum is our gluten. It is purchased in powdered or pebble form. A single tablespoon was used in most of these recipes for convenience. If you want to conserve xanthan gum, use 2½ teaspoons in a recipe and see if you can tell the difference.

Yeast comes in a variety of forms. Active yeast, Quick Rise Yeast, Bread Machine Yeast and SAF Perfect Rise ™ yeast were used throughout these recipes. Each recipe Tester had his/her own favorite. Determine which yeast you like best. Then run a test loaf to determine if your bread machine or oven requires 2, 2¼ or 2½ teaspoons of yeast in order to create your desired results.

Gelatin, unflavored, is a powder that may be added to any bread recipe for added protein. When we added 1½ teaspoons to the dry ingredients, we received mixed reviews on the results. Some people thought the bread was more elastic, while others interpreted it as spongy or rubbery.

Your Favorite Flour Mix may be used in these recipes. We suggest you use mixes that resemble the mixture in the recipe. When substituting flour mixes for the flours in the original recipe, you may need to adjust the liquid ratio. The difference in flours may also vary the taste from the original taste-tested recipe.

Make Your Own Mix with the flours and starches you find most favorable. We suggest you combine a rice flour with at last two different starches. Then add a nutritious flour, such as bean or amaranth. Or, simply save a step by combining two starches together, i.e. potato and tapioca starch and use them as one. This eliminates the need for pulling out two separate starches. There are a wide combination of mixes you can create. We suggest you try working with the flours listed in the recipes so you may determine which results you like best before making your own mix.

Your Notes

Basic to Bold Breads

Abbreviated Baking Methods

One Step Method—Bread Machine—Time: 3½ hours
- Place ingredients into bread pan in order recommended by manufacturer.
- Select Basic and then press Start.

Two Step Method—Bread Machine—Time: 2½ hours
- Place ingredients into bread pan in order recommended by manufacturer.
- Select Dough and then press Start. Allow to mix, knead and rise.
- At end of Dough cycle, select Bake and then press Start. Bake 60-75 minutes.

No-Knead No-Rise Method—Bread Machine—Time: 1½ hours
- Add 1 tsp. baking soda and 1 Tbsp. baking powder to dry ingredients.
- Place ingredients into bread pan in order recommended by manufacturer.
- Select any mode that will mix the ingredients (i.e. Basic), then press Start.
- Mix the ingredients until well blended, 5-7 minutes, then press Stop.
- Select Bake and then press Start. There is no rise time. Bake 60-75 minutes.

For all methods, assist in mixing and make any necessary liquid adjustments.
For detailed bread machine instructions, see pages 125 through 129.

Oven Method
- You may bake all the recipes in this book in the oven. First, determine how you want to mix, knead and/or rise the ingredients. Then decide if you want the bread to rise before baking, or use the No-Knead No-Rise method.

For detailed oven instructions, see pages 130 through 132.

My Personalized Recipe for: ....

Date:________________ Baking method used:________________________

Amount and type of liquid used:______________________________

Flours or mix used:_____________________________________

Other changes:____

Notes:____

____

When personalizing with different flours or ingredients to suit your tastes, diet, for convenience, or for creativity, you may need to adjust the other ingredients.

My Personalized Recipe for: . . . .

Date:________________ Baking method used:________________________

Amount and type of liquid used:_____________________________________

Flours or mix used:____

Other changes:____

Notes:____

____

My Personalized Recipe for: . . . .

Date:________________ Baking method used:________________________

Amount and type of liquid used:_____________________________________

Flours or mix used:____

Other changes:____

Notes:____

____

My Personalized Recipe for: . . . .

Date:________________ Baking method used:________________________

Amount and type of liquid used:_____________________________________

Flours or mix used:____

Other changes:____

Notes:____

____

When personalizing with different flours or ingredients to suit your tastes, diet, for convenience, or for creativity, you may need to adjust the other ingredients.

Apple Bread

An excellent bread using simple ingredients in a gluten-free kitchen.

Wet Ingredients: (see page 6)

¾ cup	eggs
½ cup	chunky applesauce
¾ cup	apple juice, plus or minus
1 teaspoon	cider vinegar
1 teaspoon	vanilla extract
1 Tablespoon	vegetable oil
¾ cup	freshly grated apple
¾ cup	golden raisins

***Hint:** Grate the washed apple with or without the skin.*

Dry Ingredients: (see page 7)

2 cups	white rice flour
½ cup	tapioca starch flour
½ cup	cornstarch

—or *personalize with your favorite flour mix*—

1 teaspoon	salt
1 Tablespoon	sugar
½ cup	dry milk powder
1 Tablespoon	xanthan gum
2 teaspoons	cinnamon
2½ teaspoons	yeast

***Tip:** Any applesauce will work—smooth, chunky, homemade, with or without sugar.*

For Baking Methods, see pages 125-132.

Two Additional Bread Recipes:

Apple Date Bread: Change the Apple Bread recipe as follows:

- Use ¾ cup chopped pitted dates instead of ¾ cup grated apple and add 1 teaspoon orange zest.

Apple Pear Bread: Change the Apple Bread recipe as follows:

- Use ½ cup of milk instead of the ½ cup applesauce.
- Use 1 Tablespoon brown sugar instead of 1 Tablespoon white sugar.
- Add 1 teaspoon nutmeg and ¼ teaspoon ginger.
- Use a mixture of dried pears and dried apples to equal ¾ cup instead of ¾ cup freshly grated apple.

Basic Sandwich Bread

"This will remind you of wheat white breads," says Sarah F. Day, the contributor of this wonderful recipe. It works equally well in the bread machine or oven, as a loaf bread, rolls or buns.

Hint: The recipe is a smaller loaf than others in this book so you can make it fresh more often.

Wet Ingredients: (see page 6)

2	eggs
3 Tablespoons	milk or water, plus or minus
1 cup	unflavored, unsweetened yogurt
¼ cup	vegetable oil or oil of your choice
1 teaspoon	rice or cider vinegar

Dry Ingredients: (see page 7)

¼ cup	white rice flour
1 Tablespoon	brown rice flour or millet flour
½ cup	tapioca starch flour
½ cup	potato starch
¾ cup	cornstarch
½ teaspoon	baking soda
1 Tablespoon	baking powder
2 Tablespoons	white or brown sugar
½ teaspoon	salt
2 teaspoons	xanthan gum
3 Tablespoons	cornmeal (optional)
1 Tablespoon	yeast

Tip: If desired, add 1 Tablespoon Italian herbs to dry ingredients for a different flavor.

***FYI**: Due to the recipe size, this may be mixed by hand for approximately 3-5 minutes. The dough will be on the thick side. If you have difficulties mixing by hand, use a hand or stand mixer. Do not over mix.*

When using the bread machine, mix for 6–8 minutes. You may need to help it mix to get the ingredients fully combined together within a short period of time.

It is important to mix the dough as quickly as possible when using the No-Knead No-Rise Method of baking. The baking powder/baking soda/yeast mixture helps the bread to rise, but their power dissipates if it takes too long to get the bread into the oven.

Bake bread or rolls at 350°. Bread takes approximately 1 hour, and the rolls 35–45 minutes, depending on their size.

Caramel Rolls: Before preparing the bread dough, make the caramel topping. Combine the following in a sauce pan and heat until it starts to bubble:

¼ cup	brown sugar
1 Tablespoon	light corn syrup
2 Tablespoons	unsalted butter
1 teaspoon	vanilla extract
a sprinkle of	cinnamon
¼ cup chopped	walnuts or pecans

Pour the caramel topping into 10 muffin tins. Allow to cool while you prepare the dough. After you have baked the muffins 35-45 minutes, remove from oven and place on wire rack. Turn the pan upside down and allow the caramel topping to drip down the muffins. After 5-7 minutes, remove the pan and allow rolls to cool.

Cinnamon Rolls: Everyone likes their cinnamon rolls a little different. Some people like lots of cinnamon and very little sugar, and others like it the other way around. Our idea is to simply combine equal amounts of cinnamon and sugar into the bottom of each muffin tin. Then place your dough over the cinnamon and sugar and bake. Frost with Cream Cheese Frosting.

Cream Cheese Frosting:

½ pkg. (2 cups)	powdered sugar
1 Tablespoon	evaporated milk
¼ cup	butter, melted
4 ounce (½ cup)	cream cheese, softened

With an electric mixer, combine all of the powdered sugar and melted butter and enough evaporated or regular milk to make a stiff frosting. Add softened cream cheese and mix on high for 1 minute. Add more milk for preferred consistency.

Brown Rice Bread

Looking for a tasty basic bread that will not compete with the flavor of the toppings? This is it! Bake one up tonight.

Wet Ingredients: (see page 6)

¾ cup	eggs
¾ cup	water, plus or minus
½ teaspoon	vanilla extract
1 teaspoon	cider vinegar
½ cup	applesauce
3 Tablespoons	light molasses

Hint: *This bread bakes up nicely using the No-Knead No-Rise Method.*

Dry Ingredients: (see page 7)

2 cup	brown rice flour
½ cup	cornstarch
½ cup	tapioca starch flour

—or personalize with your favorite flour mix—

1 teaspoon	salt
2 Tablespoons	dry milk powder
2 teaspoons	xanthan gum
2 ½ teaspoons	yeast

Veggie Sandwich: See "Beyond Bread" section, page 141.

Honey Walnut Spread: See "Beyond Bread" section, page 138.

Additional Bread Recipe

Brown Rice & Sage Bread: To the above Brown Rice Bread recipe, add:

- 2 teaspoons celery seed
- 1 Tablespoon dried rubbed sage
- 2 Tablespoons finely chopped parsley
- ½ cup sweet onion cooked until tender in 1 Tablespoon butter, then cooled.

FYI: *Dried Rubbed Sage is sage crumbled and ground into a powder. Or break Dried Sage pieces between your fingers and rub to release their aroma and potency.*

Brown Rice Brown Rice Bread

"This easy-to-make bread is enjoyable to eat."–Marie

Wet Ingredients: (see page 6)

¾ cup	eggs
¾ cup	water, plus or minus
½ teaspoon	vanilla extract
1 teaspoon	cider vinegar
½ cup	applesauce
3 Tablespoons	gluten-free brown rice syrup
½ cup	precooked, cooled brown rice

Dry Ingredients: (see page 7)

2 cup	brown rice flour
½ cup	cornstarch
½ cup	potato starch

–or personalize with your favorite flour mix–

1 teaspoon	salt
2 Tablespoons	dry milk powder
2 teaspoons	xanthan gum
2½ teaspoons	yeast

***Hint:** Make enough brown rice so you have leftovers. Add them to your meatloaf or as a side dish for dinner. Or warm cooked rice in the microwave and add nuts, seeds and raisins for a quick morning breakfast.*

***Tip:** Brown rice syrup is an extremely versatile and relatively healthy sweetener made from brown rice through an enzymatic process. Either verify it is gluten-free or substitute maple syrup or light molasses.*

***FYI:** Brown rice, because it is the entire grain without the outer husk, takes slightly longer to cook than white rice. Regular, Quick and Instant brown rice will all work in this recipe. If you like being able to see the pieces of rice in the bread–and we do–do not overcook the rice.*

For Baking Methods, see pages 125-132.

Cinnamon Raisin Bread

This Cinnamon Raisin Bread with the cinnamon sugar filling is fabulous."—Linda

Wet Ingredients: (see page 6)

¾ cup	eggs
¾ cup	apple juice
½ cup	water, plus or minus
1 teaspoon	cider vinegar
1 teaspoon	vanilla extract
2 Tablespoons	applesauce

Dry Ingredients: (see page 7)

2 cups	white rice flour
½ cup	tapioca starch flour
½ cup	cornstarch

—or personalize with your favorite flour mix—

1 teaspoon	salt
¼ cup	light brown sugar
½ cup	dry milk powder
1 Tablespoon	xanthan gum
2 teaspoons	cinnamon
2½ teaspoons	yeast

Add in:

1 cup	raisins
½ cup	chopped walnuts

***FYI:** Korintje Cassia Cinnamon is sweet and mellow.*

China Cassia Cinnamon is strong, has more depth and is spicier than Korintje.

Extra Fancy Vietnamese Cinnamon is said to be the highest quality, strongest cinnamon available in America today.

Cinnamon and Sugar Filling and Topping: Combine together ½ cup sugar, 1 teaspoon cinnamon, 2 Tablespoons of very soft butter and a teaspoon of molasses. Cut this combination into the bread using a butter knife, and also spread on top. If you are using one of the rise methods, cut in after the bread has risen. If you are using the No-Knead, No-Bake Method, cut in after mixing and before baking the bread.

Citrus Zest Bread

"Best gluten-free bread I have ever tasted!"–Sheila

Wet Ingredients: (see page 6)

¾ cup	eggs
¾ cup	apple juice, plus or minus
¾ cup	orange juice concentrate, thawed
3 Tablespoons	vegetable oil
1 teaspoon	cider vinegar
1 teaspoon	fresh squeezed lime juice
1 teaspoon	fresh squeezed lemon juice

Dry Ingredients: (see page 7)

1 cup	white rice flour
½ cup	potato starch
¼ cup	tapioca starch flour
1 cup	millet flour
¼ cup	sweet rice flour

–or personalize with your favorite flour mix–

1 teaspoon	salt
3 Tablespoons	sugar
1 Tablespoon	xanthan gum
2 Tablespoons	orange zest
1 teaspoon	lemon zest
½ teaspoon	lime zest
2½ teaspoons	yeast

Hint: *Remove the peel (zest) of the lemon, orange and lime, without removing the white bitter pith by using a vegetable peeler, or special graters called "zesters".*

Mandarin Orange Spread: See "Beyond Bread" section, page 138.

For
Baking Methods,
see pages 125-132.

Cream of Rice™ Bread

"Cream of Rice™ is a comfort food in our home. It adds texture to this bread."–Marie

Wet Ingredients: (see page 6)

¾ cup	eggs
1 cup	apple juice, plus or minus
1 teaspoon	rice vinegar
¼ cup	applesauce
1 teaspoon	vanilla extract
1 mashed	banana

Dry Ingredients: (see page 7)

1 cup	white rice flour
1 cup	brown rice flour
½ cup	tapioca starch flour
½ cup	potato starch flour

–or personalize with your favorite flour mix–

¼ cup	sweet rice flour
¼ cup	Cream of Rice™ cereal
1 teaspoon	salt
1 Tablespoon	sugar
2 Tablespoons	dry milk powder
1 Tablespoon	xanthan gum
1 teaspoon	cinnamon
2½ teaspoons	yeast

Egg-in-Hole Breakfast Entree: See "Beyond Bread" section, page 137.

For
Baking Methods,
see pages 125-132.

Dill and Cottage Cheese Bread

"Thank you, Mindy, for sharing one of your favorite family recipes–converted to gluten-free."–LynnRae

Wet Ingredients: (see page 6)

¾ cup	eggs
¾ cup	water, plus or minus
1 teaspoon	cider vinegar
2 Tablespoons	unsalted butter, melted
1 cup	small curd cottage cheese

Dry Ingredients: (see page 7)

1 cup	white rice flour
1 cup	brown rice flour
½ cup	cornstarch
½ cup	tapioca starch flour

–or personalize with your favorite flour mix–

1 teaspoon	salt
¼ cup	sugar
¼ cup	dry milk powder
2 Tablespoons	dry minced onion
2 Tablespoons	dill weed
1 Tablespoon	xanthan gum
2½ teaspoons	yeast

Hint: *Dill Weed is similar to Dill Seed but they are not interchangeable in most recipes. Dill Weed, the dried leaves part of the plant, is mellower and fresher in flavor.*

FYI: *Dill Seed and Dill Weed are used in pickling as well as in German, Russian and Scandinavian dishes. According to an Old Norse tale, Dill was used to lull babies to sleep and as an antidote to witchcraft.*

Crab & Dill Spread: See "Beyond Bread" section, page 136.

"The refreshing flavor of this bread is perfect when topped with sour cream and chives." –Kitten

Mashed Potato and Cheese Bread

The mild taste of this bread is just what you want for a basic sandwich bread.

Tip: Use the water from boiling the potatoes. It will help the bread rise.

Hint: You can pre-season the potatoes by boiling them in chicken broth, adding garlic cloves to the potato water, or incorporating butter into the mashed potatoes before adding to the bread.

Wet Ingredients: (see page 6)

¾ cup	eggs
1 cup	potato water, plus or minus
1 teaspoon	rice vinegar
2 teaspoons	unsalted butter, melted
½ cup	fluffy mashed potatoes
2 Tablespoons	light corn syrup

Dry Ingredients: (see page 7)

½ cup	white rice flour
1 cup	brown rice flour
½ cup	cornstarch
½ cup	potato starch
½ cup	millet flour
2 Tablespoons	sweet rice flour

—or personalize with your favorite flour mix—

1 teaspoon	onion salt (not onion power)
2 Tablespoons	egg replacer
1 Tablespoon	xanthan gum
2½ teaspoons	yeast

Add in:

½ cup	shredded pepper jack cheese

***FYI:** Perfect for leftover mashed potatoes.*

Grilled Tomato, Avocado and Muenster Sandwich: See "Beyond Bread" section, page 137.

Rice and White Rice Bread

As kids, we would toast our favorite white bread and cover it with a cream of mushroom or celery soup. Sometimes Mom would add sausage for a heartier meal. Share some of those same memories by spooning Mushroom and Asparagus Duxelle over toasted bread.

Wet Ingredients: (see page 6)

¾ cup	eggs
1 cup	water, plus or minus
3 Tablespoons	vegetable oil
1 teaspoon	vinegar
1 cup	room temperature cooked, drained, white rice

Dry Ingredients: (see page 7)

2 cups	white rice flour
½ cup	tapioca starch flour
½ cup	cornstarch

—or personalize with your favorite flour mix—

1 teaspoon	salt
2 Tablespoons	sugar
½ cup	dry milk powder
2 teaspoons	xanthan gum
2½ teaspoons	yeast

***Hint**: Instant, par-broiled, long grain or short grain white rice will all work in this recipe.*

***Tip**: Sweet rice (sticky rice) is not necessarily recommended for this recipe, unless you want to turn the bread into an appetizer or dumpling that may benefit from the added "stickiness".*

Mushroom and Asparagus Duxelle Entree: See "Beyond Bread," page 139.

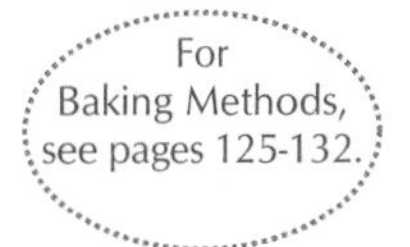
For
Baking Methods,
see pages 125-132.

Roasted Garlic Bread

"I could eat this bread all day. It is even better toasted." –Yvonne

Wet Ingredients: (see page 6)

¾ cup	eggs
¾ cup	water, plus or minus
3 Tablespoons	olive oil
1 teaspoon	vinegar
¼ cup	roasted garlic, about 2 heads

Dry Ingredients: (see page 7)

1 cup	white rice flour
1 cup	brown rice flour
½ cup	tapioca starch flour
½ cup	cornstarch

—or personalize with your favorite flour mix—

1 teaspoon	garlic salt
3 Tablespoons	sugar
2 Tablespoons	dry milk powder
1 Tablespoon	xanthan gum
1 teaspoon	dough enhancer
2½ teaspoons	yeast

***Tip:** Dough enhancer is recommended to help the rise in this recipe.*

How to Roast a Head of Garlic: Preheat oven to 350°. Break garlic head into cloves. Place unpeeled cloves in small oven-proof container and toss with ½ cup extra virgin olive oil. Season lightly with salt and pepper. Add a sprig of rosemary or thyme to the container. Cover and bake until tender, 30 to 40 minutes. Remove from oven and cool. Squeeze the garlic out of the paper.

***FYI:** White parchment-skin garlic has a strong garlic flavor that turns sweet when roasted. Elephant garlic is not true garlic. It is of the leek family and has a mild, delicate sweet taste that is even milder when roasted.*

Sour Cream and Chives Bread

"I loved the deliciously soft texture of this bread and its mild but rich flavor. It was easy to build a tuna fish sandwich around it."—Denise

Wet Ingredients: (see page 6)

¾ cup	eggs
¾ cup	potato water, plus or minus
1 teaspoon	cider vinegar
3 Tablespoons	olive oil
¾ cup	sour cream
2 Tablespoons	chopped chives

Dry Ingredients: (see page 7)

2 cups	white rice flour
½ cup	tapioca starch flour
½ cup	cornstarch
—or personalize with your favorite flour mix—	
1 teaspoon	salt
3 Tablespoons	sugar
½ cup	dry milk powder
2 teaspoons	xanthan gum
½ cup	instant potato flakes
2½ teaspoons	yeast

Tip: *Chives are an herb with a delicate onion flavor that may be purchased fresh, frozen or freeze-dried. You may substitute green onion for the chives, knowing the onion will have a stronger taste.*

Tuna Nicoise Sandwich: See "Beyond Bread" section, page 141.

For Baking Methods, see pages 125-132.

My Personalized Recipe for: ....

Date:________________ Baking method used:________________________

Amount and type of liquid used:________________________________

Flours or mix used:____

Other changes:____

Notes:____

____

My Personalized Recipe for: ....

Date:________________ Baking method used:________________________

Amount and type of liquid used:________________________________

Flours or mix used:____

Other changes:____

Notes:____

____

My Personalized Recipe for: ....

Date:________________ Baking method used:________________________

Amount and type of liquid used:________________________________

Flours or mix used:____

Other changes:____

Notes:____

____

When personalizing with different flours or ingredients to suit your tastes, diet, for convenience, or for creativity, you may need to adjust the other ingredients.

Meal-in-a-Slice Breads

Abbreviated Baking Methods

One Step Method—Bread Machine—Time: 3½ hours

- Place ingredients into bread pan in order recommended by manufacturer.
- Select Basic and then press Start.

Two Step Method—Bread Machine—Time: 2½ hours

- Place ingredients into bread pan in order recommended by manufacturer.
- Select Dough and then press Start. Allow to mix, knead and rise.
- At end of Dough cycle, select Bake and then press Start. Bake 60-75 minutes.

No-Knead No-Rise Method—Bread Machine—Time: 1½ hours

- Add 1 tsp. baking soda and 1 Tbsp. baking powder to dry ingredients.
- Place ingredients into bread pan in order recommended by manufacturer.
- Select any mode that will mix the ingredients (i.e. Basic), then press Start.
- Mix the ingredients until well blended, 5-7 minutes, then press Stop.
- Select Bake and then press Start. There is no rise time. Bake 60-75 minutes.

For all methods, assist in mixing and make any necessary liquid adjustments.
For detailed bread machine instructions, see pages 125 through 129.

Oven Method

- You may bake all the recipes in this book in the oven. First, determine how you want to mix, knead and/or rise the ingredients. Then decide if you want the bread to rise before baking, or use the No-Knead No-Rise method.

For detailed oven instructions, see pages 130 through 132.

My Personalized Recipe for: . . . .

Date:________________ Baking method used:______________________________

Amount and type of liquid used:______________________________________

Flours or mix used:____

Other changes:____

Notes:____

____

When personalizing with different flours or ingredients to suit your tastes, diet, for convenience, or for creativity, you may need to adjust the other ingredients.

My Personalized Recipe for: . . . .

Date:________________ Baking method used:____________________________

Amount and type of liquid used:____

Flours or mix used:____

Other changes:____

Notes:____

____

My Personalized Recipe for: . . . .

Date:________________ Baking method used:____________________________

Amount and type of liquid used:____

Flours or mix used:____

Other changes:____

Notes:____

____

My Personalized Recipe for: . . . .

Date:________________ Baking method used:____________________________

Amount and type of liquid used:____

Flours or mix used:____

Other changes:____

Notes:____

____

When personalizing with different flours or ingredients to suit your tastes, diet, for convenience, or for creativity, you may need to adjust the other ingredients.

Bacon and Eggs Bread

"One of my favorites for 'Breakfast on the Road'."—Vern

Wet Ingredients: (see page 6)

¾ cup	eggs
1 cup	water, plus or minus
1 teaspoon	vinegar
2 Tablespoons	pure maple syrup
½ cup	grated, sharp cheddar cheese
½ cup	cooked, drained, cooled and crumbled bacon

Dry Ingredients: (see page 7)

1 cup	white rice flour
1 cup	brown rice flour
¼ cup	tapioca starch flour
¼ cup	potato starch
½ cup	quinoa flour

—or personalize with your favorite flour mix—

1 teaspoon	salt
¼ cup	dry milk powder
1 Tablespoon	xanthan gum
1 Tablespoon	yeast

***Hint:** Turkey bacon or precooked sausage may also be used.*

***Tip:** Add 1 Tablespoon of bacon grease to the wet ingredients, if desired.*

***Recommendation:** This recipe works best when allowed to rise before baking. **FYI:** Keep refrigerated or frozen.*

Bacon and Egg Salad Entree: See "Beyond Bread," page 135.

For Baking Methods, see pages 125-132.

Cheese and Franks Bread

"Yum! Great idea!"—Hannah

Wet Ingredients: (see page 6)

¾ cup	eggs
¾ cup	potato water, plus or minus
1 teaspoon	vinegar
¼ cup	oil
3 Tablespoons	sweet pickle relish

***Hint:** A mustard relish may be used instead of the pickle relish.*

Dry Ingredients: (see page 7)

1 cup	white rice flour
¼ cup	sweet rice flour
¼ cup	tapioca starch flour
½ cup	potato starch
½ cup	cornstarch
½ cup	millet flour

—or personalize with your favorite flour mix—

1 teaspoon	salt
3 Tablespoons	sugar
½ cup	dry milk powder
1 Tablespoon	xanthan gum
1 Tablespoon	egg replacer
¼ teaspoon	ground ginger
2 teaspoons	dry or prepared mustard
2½ teaspoons	yeast

***Tip:** Cut the franks into small pieces. Too large of pieces will prevent the bread from holding together.*

Add in:

½ cup	grated sharp cheddar cheese
1 cup	cut up precooked franks

***Recommendation:** This recipe works best when allowed to rise before baking. **FYI:** Keep refrigerated or frozen.*

Quick Potato Salad: See "Beyond Bread," page 140.

Chicken & Peppers Bread

The aroma of this freshly baked bread will have you hanging around the kitchen in anticipation.

Wet Ingredients: (see page 6)

¾ cup	eggs
¾ cup	water, plus or minus
1 teaspoon	cider vinegar
½ cup	mayonnaise
2 crushed	garlic cloves

Hint: *For added nutrition, flavor, and color add 1 small jar of Chicken and Rice Baby Food.*

Dry Ingredients: (see page 7)

1 cup	white rice flour
½ cup	brown rice flour
½ cup	cornstarch
½ cup	potato starch
½ cup	millet flour

—or personalize with your favorite flour mix—

1 teaspoon	onion salt
1 Tablespoon	sugar
1 Tablespoon	xanthan gum
2 teaspoons	egg replacer
2½ teaspoons	yeast

Tip: *You may use salad dressing instead of mayonnaise. According to Food Lover's Companion by Barron's, mayonnaise contains egg yolks. Salad dressing does not. Salad dressing is sweeter than mayonnaise.*

Add in:

¾ cup	cooked and diced chicken
½ cup	diced green peppers

Recommendation: *This recipe works best when allowed to rise before baking.* ***FYI:*** *Keep refrigerated or frozen.*

Easy Mexican Rice: See "Beyond Bread," page 137.

For Baking Methods, see pages 125-132.

Deli Style Ham & Cheese Bread

Now you can create your own award-winning muffuletta-deli-style sandwich.

Wet Ingredients: (see page 6)

¾ cup	eggs
¾ cup	water, plus or minus
1 teaspoon	cider vinegar
¼ cup	mayonnaise
2 Tablespoons	coarsely ground mustard
2 teaspoons	pickle relish

Dry Ingredients: (see page 7)

1 cup	white rice flour
1 cup	brown rice flour
¼ cup	cornstarch
½ cup	garfava bean flour
¼ cup	sweet rice flour

—or personalize with your favorite flour mix—

1 teaspoon	salt
¼ cup	brown sugar
½ cup	dry milk powder
1 Tablespoon	xanthan gum
2 teaspoons	caraway seeds
2½ teaspoons	yeast

Add in:

¾ cup	finely diced pre-cooked ham
1 cup	shredded Swiss cheese

Hint: *The ham will be easier to slice if it is cold.*

Tip: *Pickle relish can be substituted with hot dog relish, corn relish, or a smooth, sweet chutney.*

Recommendation: *This recipe works best when allowed to rise before baking.* ***FYI:*** *Keep refrigerated or frozen.*

Onion Muffuletta Sandwich: See "Beyond Bread," page 139.

Ham and Cheese Bread

For breakfast, Chef Tanya recommends it grilled and served with an egg on top.

Wet Ingredients: (see page 6)

3/4 cup	eggs
3/4 cup	potato water, plus or minus
1 teaspoon	cider vinegar
2 Tablespoons	vegetable oil
2 Tablespoons	light molasses
2 Tablespoons	prepared mustard

Dry Ingredients: (see page 7)

1 cup	white rice flour
1 cup	brown rice flour
1/4 cup	cornstarch
1/2 cup	garfava bean flour
1/4 cup	sweet rice flour

—or personalize with your favorite flour mix—

1 teaspoon	salt
1/4 cup	brown sugar
1/2 cup	dry milk powder
1 Tablespoon	xanthan gum
2 1/2 teaspoons	yeast

Add in:

3/4 cup	diced pre-cooked ham
1 cup	shredded Swiss cheese

***Tip**: For a great hors d'oeuvres, quarter each slice, top with a sliver of ham and cheese, add an olive on top, tuck under the broiler until the cheese begins to melt, and serve hot from the broiler.—Linda*

***Recommendation:** This recipe works best when allowed to rise before baking. **FYI:** Keep refrigerated or frozen.*

Chopped Ham Spread: See "Beyond Bread," page 136.

For Baking Methods, see pages 125-132.

Peanut Butter and Banana Bread

"This bread is great. It makes an excellent peanut butter and honey toast."–Denise

Hint: *Spray the inside of the measuring cup with a vegetable oil before measuring the peanut butter, for an easier clean-up.*

Wet Ingredients: (see page 6)

3/4 cup	eggs
3/4 cup	water, plus or minus
1 teaspoon	vinegar
2 Tablespoons	honey
1 teaspoon	vanilla extract
1/2 cup	chunky style peanut butter
1 cup	mashed banana

Dry Ingredients: (see page 7)

1 cup	white rice flour
1/2 cup	tapioca starch flour
1/2 cup	cornstarch
1/2 cup	sweet rice flour
1/2 cup	quinoa flour
–or personalize with your favorite flour mix–	
1 teaspoon	salt
1/2 cup	dry milk powder
2 teaspoons	xanthan gum
1/2 teaspoon	cinnamon
2 1/2 teaspoons	yeast

Tip: *If allergic to peanuts or would like to try something new, try almond or cashew butters.*

Recommendation: *Allow to rise before baking.* ***FYI:*** *Keep refrigerated or frozen.*

Peanut Butter Glaze: See "Beyond Bread," page 139.

Additional Bread Recipe:

Peanut Butter and Jelly Bread:

- Substitute millet flour for the quinoa flour and use 1/2 cup apricot jelly instead of the mashed banana.

Pizza Slice Bread

"It smells like the real thing and tastes even better."—Brian
"It's easy to microwave for a quick pizza."—Tess

Wet Ingredients: (see page 6)

3/4 cup	eggs
1 cup	tomato juice, plus or minus
1/4 teaspoon	red wine vinegar
1/4 cup	olive oil
1 Tablespoon	tomato paste

Dry Ingredients: (see page 7)

1 1/2 cups	white rice flour
1/2 cup	tapioca starch flour
1/4 cup	potato starch
1/4 cup	cornstarch
1/4 cup	sweet rice flour
1/2 cup	millet flour

—or personalize with your favorite flour mix—

1 teaspoon	salt
3 Tablespoons	sugar
2/3 cups	dry milk powder
1 Tablespoon	xanthan gum
2 teaspoons	egg replacer (optional)
2 1/2 teaspoons	yeast

Add in:

1/2 cup	finely chopped, cooked gluten-free sausage
1/2 cup	finely chopped cooked pepperoni
1/2 cup	grated Parmesan cheese

Hint: *Tomato paste is made from tomatoes and is available in cans or in tubes. Tubes allow you to use only what you need and refrigerate the rest.*

Tip: *Use this recipe as a stuffed pizza crust.*

For
Baking Methods,
see pages 125-132.

Recommendation: *This recipe works best when allowed to rise before baking.* ***FYI:*** *Keep refrigerated or frozen.*

Pizza Appetizer/Entree: See "Beyond Bread," page 139.

Reuben Bread

"One of the best recipes in this book. Hands-down first place!"—Kathy.

Tip: *Use the sauerkraut liquid instead of the water.*

Hint: *If you cannot find a gluten-free Thousand Island Salad Dressing on your grocery market shelves, and you do not want to make your own, simply use ½ cup mayonnaise.*

Wet Ingredients: (see page 6)

¾ cup	eggs
½ cup	water, plus or minus
¼ cup	olive oil
2 Tablespoons	light molasses
½ cup	Thousand Island Salad Dressing
1 cup	sauerkraut, drained and chopped

Dry Ingredients: (see page 7)

1¾ cups	white rice flour
1 cup	brown rice flour
¼ cup	sweet rice flour

—or personalize with your favorite flour mix—

1 Tablespoon	sorghum flour
1 teaspoon	salt
¼ cup	brown sugar
½ cup	dry milk powder
1 Tablespoon	xanthan gum
1 Tablespoon	caraway seeds
2½ teaspoons	yeast

Add in:

1 cup	diced, fresh corned beef, not canned
½ cup	shredded Swiss cheese

Recommendation: *This recipe works best when allowed to rise before baking.* ***FYI:*** *Keep refrigerated or frozen.*

Thousand Island Salad Dressing: See "Beyond Bread," page 141.

"Thank you for being daring and creative enough to make this recipe! The taste is outstanding."—Tanya

Turkey and Cranberry Bread

"Very flavorful. We ate it plain as a compliment to a hearty soup."—Jeanne

Wet Ingredients: (see page 6)

3/4 cup	eggs
1/2 cup	water, plus or minus
1 teaspoon	rice vinegar
1/2 cup	mayonnaise
1/2 cup	whole canned cranberries, drained

Dry Ingredients: (see page 7)

1 cup	white rice flour
1/2 cup	brown rice flour
1/2 cup	potato starch
1/2 cup	tapioca starch flour
1/2 cup	cornstarch

—or personalize with your favorite flour mix—

1 teaspoon	salt
2 Tablespoons	sugar
1/2 cup	dry milk powder
1 Tablespoon	egg replacer
1 Tablespoon	xanthan gum
2 1/2 teaspoons	yeast

Add in:

3/4 cup	diced precooked turkey
1/4 cup	shredded Swiss cheese

Hint: *This bread was originally made using quinoa flour. Some Tasters said the quinoa overtook the fragile taste of the turkey, so the lighter flours and starches were used. If the taste of the turkey is secondary to you, use quinoa or amaranth flour for more nutrition.*

Recommendation: *This recipe works best when allowed to rise before baking.* ***FYI****: Keep refrigerated or frozen.*

Ginger Spread: See "Beyond Bread," page 137.

Orange-Cranberry Sauce: See "Beyond Bread," page 139.

For
Baking Methods,
see pages 125-132.

My Personalized Recipe for: ....

Date:________________ Baking method used:________________________

Amount and type of liquid used:____________________________________

Flours or mix used:____

Other changes:____

Notes:____

____

My Personalized Recipe for: ....

Date:________________ Baking method used:________________________

Amount and type of liquid used:____________________________________

Flours or mix used:____

Other changes:____

Notes:____

____

My Personalized Recipe for: ....

Date:________________ Baking method used:________________________

Amount and type of liquid used:____________________________________

Flours or mix used:____

Other changes:____

Notes:____

____

When personalizing with different flours or ingredients to suit your tastes, diet, for convenience, or for creativity, you may need to adjust the other ingredients.

Robust Rye Breads

Rye Bread 53

This mild gluten-free rye bread enhances the ingredients you tuck into your sandwich. It makes a great grilled cheese and is an extremely popular bread recipe. Its versatility is almost limitless.

Walnut Rye Bread. 53

Sauerkraut Rye Bread. 54

Beautiful, dark and somewhat tangy. You will be pleasantly surprised with the taste, texture and tantalizing aromas of this bread. Perfect with a pork chop and sauerkraut dinner, or as a pork sandwich.

Abbreviated Baking Methods

One Step Method—Bread Machine—Time: 3½ hours

- Place ingredients into bread pan in order recommended by manufacturer.
- Select Basic and then press Start.

Two Step Method—Bread Machine—Time: 2½ hours

- Place ingredients into bread pan in order recommended by manufacturer.
- Select Dough and then press Start. Allow to mix, knead and rise.
- At end of Dough cycle, select Bake and then press Start. Bake 60-75 minutes.

No-Knead No-Rise Method—Bread Machine—Time: 1½ hours

- Add 1 tsp. baking soda and 1 Tbsp. baking powder to dry ingredients.
- Place ingredients into bread pan in order recommended by manufacturer.
- Select any mode that will mix the ingredients (i.e. Basic), then press Start.
- Mix the ingredients until well blended, 5-7 minutes, then press Stop.
- Select Bake and then press Start. There is no rise time. Bake 60-75 minutes.

For all methods, assist in mixing and make any necessary liquid adjustments.
For detailed bread machine instructions, see pages 125 through 129.

Oven Method

- You may bake all the recipes in this book in the oven. First, determine how you want to mix, knead and/or rise the ingredients. Then decide if you want the bread to rise before baking, or use the No-Knead No-Rise method.

For detailed oven instructions, see pages 130 through 132.

My Personalized Recipe for: . . . .

Date:________________ Baking method used:______________________________

Amount and type of liquid used:____

Flours or mix used:____

Other changes:____

Notes:____

____

When personalizing with different flours or ingredients to suit your tastes, diet, for convenience, or for creativity, you may need to adjust the other ingredients.

My Personalized Recipe for: . . . .

Date:________________ Baking method used:____________________

Amount and type of liquid used:________________________________

Flours or mix used:_______________________________________

Other changes:____

Notes:____

____

My Personalized Recipe for: . . . .

Date:________________ Baking method used:____________________

Amount and type of liquid used:________________________________

Flours or mix used:_______________________________________

Other changes:____

Notes:____

____

My Personalized Recipe for: . . . .

Date:________________ Baking method used:____________________

Amount and type of liquid used:________________________________

Flours or mix used:_______________________________________

Other changes:____

Notes:____

____

When personalizing with different flours or ingredients to suit your tastes, diet, for convenience, or for creativity, you may need to adjust the other ingredients.

Buckwheat Pumpernickel Bread

"Nice hearty texture and taste, like a good whole wheat bread."–Jeanne

Wet Ingredients: (see page 6)

3/4 cup	eggs
3/4 cup	water, plus or minus
1/4 cup	vegetable oil
2 Tablespoons	dark corn syrup

Hint: *Use prune juice instead of water for a healthier bread.*

Dry Ingredients: (see page 7)

2 cups	white rice flour
2/3 cup	brown rice flour
1/3 cup	buckwheat flour

—or personalize with your favorite flour mix—

1 teaspoon	salt
2 Tablespoons	dark brown sugar
1/4 cup	instant potato flakes
1 Tablespoon	xanthan gum
2 teaspoons	caramel color (optional)
2 1/2 teaspoons	yeast

Tip: *Corn syrup is made when enzymes are added to cornstarch. Dark corn syrup has caramel flavor and color added. It is stronger flavored than light corn syrup.*

FYI: *Instant potato flakes may be used in breads, to make mashed potatoes and as a thickener for your favorite sauce or soup.*

Garlic Aioli: See "Beyond Bread," page 137.

Grilled Eggplant Sandwich: See "Beyond Bread," page 137.

"Top with the puree from the Date Cumin and Coriander Bread recipe or fig preserves. Or be adventurous and top with a spicy jelly" –Marie

For Baking Methods, see pages 125-132.

Gruyere Rye Bread

"Great sandwich bread with a nice taste and texture," says Linda. "Perfect for a traditional open-faced turkey sandwich.

Wet Ingredients: (see page 6)

¾ cup	eggs
1 cup	water, plus or minus
1 teaspoon	red wine vinegar
¼ cup	olive oil
2 Tablespoons	light molasses

Dry ingredients: (see page 7)

¾ cup	white rice flour
¾ cup	brown rice flour
½ cup	potato starch or cornstarch
½ cup	tapioca starch flour
¼ cup	sweet rice flour
¼ cup	millet flour

—or personalize with your favorite flour mix—

1 teaspoon	salt
½ cup	dry milk powder
¼ cup	brown sugar
1 Tablespoon	xanthan gum
1 teaspoon	rye flavor (optional)
2½ teaspoons	yeast

Add in:

1½ cups	shredded Gruyere cheese

Hint: *Gruyere cheese is easier to grate if it is cold.*

Tip: *Change the taste with a Jarlsberg Cheese. It is sweeter and less nutty than the Gruyere cheese.*

FYI: *Gruyere cheese is frequently used for fondues, sauces and as a table cheese. Avoid the foil wrapped processed Gruyere cheese wedges and look for a round or wedge with a golden brown rind and pale yellow interior.*

Traditional Open-Faced Turkey Sandwich: See "Beyond Bread," page 141.

Limpa Rye Bread

Quinoa flour or Sorghum flour add just the right amount of texture and flavor to this bread without overpowering the delightful orange and rye.

Wet Ingredients: (see page 6)

¾ cup	eggs
1 cup	water, plus or minus
1 teaspoon	vinegar
¼ cup	olive oil
2 Tablespoons	light molasses
1 Tablespoon	honey

Dry Ingredients: (see page 7)

¾ cup	white rice flour
¾ cup	brown rice flour
¼ cup	sweet rice flour
½ cup	tapioca starch flour
½ cup	potato starch
¼ cup	quinoa flour or sorghum flour

—or personalize with your favorite flour mix—

1 teaspoon	salt
¼ cup	light brown sugar
½ cup	dry milk powder
1 Tablespoon	xanthan gum
1 Tablespoon	caraway seeds
2 teaspoons	fennel seeds
1 teaspoon	anise seeds
1 teaspoon	rye flavor (optional)
2 Tablespoons	orange zest
2½ teaspoons	yeast

FYI: *Anise seeds have a sweet, licorice flavor. Fennel seeds are sweeter than anise seeds. Caraway seeds have a slight nutty taste, and very light anise flavor.*

Swedish Meatball Sandwich: See "Beyond Bread," page 140.

Hint: *Orange, lemon or lime zest peel may be frozen for up to one month.*

Tip: *Grind the caraway, fennel and anise seeds together for a smoother bread texture.*

For Baking Methods, see pages 125-132.

Mustard Rye Bread

"Our guests enjoy this bread cut into circles, toasted, and topped with Dressed Up Mayonnaise as an appetizer."–Marie

Wet Ingredients: (see page 6)

¾ cup	eggs
1 cup	water, plus or minus
1 teaspoon	vinegar
¼ cup	olive oil
2 Tablespoons	light molasses
2 Tablespoons	honey
¼ cup	Dijon mustard

Dry Ingredients: (see page 7)

¾ cup	white rice flour
¾ cup	brown rice flour
¼ cup	sweet rice flour
½ cup	tapioca starch flour
½ cup	potato starch
¼ cup	quinoa flour

—or personalize with your favorite flour mix—

1 teaspoon	salt
¼ cup	light brown sugar
½ cup	dry milk powder
1 Tablespoon	xanthan gum
3 teaspoons	caraway seeds
1 teaspoon	brown mustard seed
1 teaspoon	yellow mustard seed
½ teaspoon	rye flavor (optional)
2½ teaspoons	yeast

Hint: *Substituting mustards will result in a different flavored bread. Dijon mustard is made with brown mustard seeds, wine and seasonings, resulting in a mild to hot mustard. American-Style mustard is made with yellow mustard seeds, sugar, vinegar and turmeric, resulting in a mild flavored mustard.*

FYI: *Yellow whole mustard seeds may be found in grocery stores. Pungent brown mustard seeds can be found in most Asian stores.*

Dressed up Mayonnaise: See "Beyond Bread," page 137.

Onion Rye Bread

Caramelize the onions to bring out their sweetness. If you truly enjoy onions, increase the amount.

Wet Ingredients: (see page 6)

¾ cup	eggs
1 cup	water, plus or minus
1 teaspoon	red wine vinegar
¼ cup	vegetable oil
2 Tablespoons	honey
¾ cup	caramelized diced red onion

Dry Ingredients: (see page 7)

¾ cup	white rice flour
¾ cup	brown rice flour
¼ cup	sweet rice flour
½ cup	tapioca starch flour
½ cup	potato starch
¼ cup	sorghum flour

—or personalize with your favorite flour mix—

1 teaspoon	onion salt
¼ cup	light brown sugar
½ cup	dry milk powder
1 Tablespoon	xanthan gum
3 teaspoons	caraway seeds
½ teaspoon	rye flavor (optional)
2½ teaspoons	yeast

Tip: *Make extra caramelized onions. When cooled, puree them to use as a gravy thickener or as part of the liquid for this bread.*

How to Caramelize Onions: *Sauté over medium heat in 2 Tablespoons of extra virgin olive oil until they are soft and brown, 15 minutes or so.*

FYI: *Onion types will create different tastes in your bread. Sweeter onions are the Maui, Vidalia, and Walla Walla. Milder flavored onions include the Bermuda, Spanish and red or Italian Onion.*

For Baking Methods, see pages 125-132.

Herb Cheese Butter: See "Beyond Bread," page 138.

Pumpernickel Bread

"One of my favorites. Very versatile."–Maurice
"I loved the moisture and caraway seeds."–Raquel
"Top this with pastrami or corned beef."–Sherry

Wet Ingredients: (see page 6)

3/4 cup	eggs
1 cup	potato water, plus or minus
1 teaspoon	vinegar
1/4 cup	olive oil
2 Tablespoons	robust molasses
2 Tablespoons	prepared espresso coffee

Hint: *1 Tablespoon espresso powder may be substituted for the prepared espresso coffee.*

Dry Ingredients: (see page 7)

2 cups	white rice flour
1 cup	brown rice flour
—or personalize with your favorite flour mix—	
1 teaspoon	salt
1/4 cup	dark brown sugar
1/2 cup	dry milk powder
1/4 cup	cocoa powder
1 Tablespoon	xanthan gum
1 Tablespoon	caraway seeds
2 teaspoons	caramel color (optional)
2 1/2 teaspoons	yeast

Tip: *Look for Caramel Color that is labeled as an "all-natural caramelized corn syrup." It will make your pumpernickel or rye loaves a deeper shade of brown.*

FYI: *Cocoa powder, like chocolate, comes from cocoa beans that have been fermented, dried and roasted, ground and dried again. Pure cocoa powder is not the same as a cocoa mix. A cocoa mix usually contains cocoa powder, dry milk powder, sugar and perhaps other ingredients.*

For
Baking Methods,
see pages 125-132.

Reuben in a Dish: See "Beyond Bread," page 140.

Rye Bread

"I loved this bread so much I never did share it with the other Tasters at work. It tastes like gluten rye bread."—Denise

Wet Ingredients: (see page 6)

¾ cup	eggs
1 cup	water, plus or minus
¼ cup	vegetable oil
1 teaspoon	red wine vinegar
2 Tablespoons	light molasses

Dry Ingredients: (see page 7)

¾ cup	white rice flour
¾ cup	brown rice flour
½ cup	tapioca starch flour
½ cup	potato starch
¼ cup	sweet rice flour
¼ cup	amaranth flour

—or personalize with your favorite flour mix—

1 teaspoon	salt
¼ cup	light brown sugar
½ cup	dry milk powder
1 Tablespoon	xanthan gum
1 Tablespoon	caraway seeds
½ teaspoon	rye flavor (optional)
2½ teaspoons	yeast

Hint: *Purchase small bread pans for mini versions of this wonderful bread. This recipe also makes exquisite hamburger buns and dinner rolls.*

Tip: *Gluten-free rye flavor is available from Authentic Foods.*

Additional Bread Recipe:

Walnut Rye Bread: Add the following to Rye Bread recipe:

- 1 teaspoon ground cardamom
- ½ cup chopped and toasted walnuts
- Substitute ¼ cup melted butter or nut oil for vegetable oil.

Grilled Pineapple, Tuna and Cheese: See "Beyond Bread," page 137.

Sauerkraut Rye Bread

"Great with cheese, fruit, and a glass of wine. Top with light mayonnaise, pastrami and lettuce."—Raquel

Tip: *Use the drained sauerkraut liquid for part of the water.*

Hint: *Crumbled crisp bacon, apples or onions are all excellent additions to this bread.*

Wet Ingredients: (see page 6)

¾ cup	eggs
1 cup	water, plus or minus
¼ cup	oil
1 teaspoon	vinegar
2 Tablespoons	robust molasses
1 cup	sauerkraut completely drained and chopped

Dry Ingredients: (see page 7)

1¾ cups	white rice flour
1 cup	brown rice flour
¼ cup	sweet rice flour
1 Tablespoon	sorghum flour

—or personalize with your favorite flour mix—

1 teaspoon	salt
¼ cup	brown sugar
½ cup	dry milk powder
½ teaspoon	rye flavor
1 Tablespoon	xanthan gum
1 Tablespoon	caraway seeds
2½ teaspoons	yeast

FYI: *Precooked sauerkraut is available in cans and jars. Fresh sauerkraut—and often the tangiest, is in delicatessens and packages in the refrigerated section of your grocery store.*

Pork Chops and Sauerkraut Entree: See "Beyond Bread," page 139.

For Baking Methods, see pages 125-132.

Regional and Traditional Breads

Abbreviated Baking Methods

One Step Method—Bread Machine—Time: 3½ hours

- Place ingredients into bread pan in order recommended by manufacturer.
- Select Basic and then press Start.

Two Step Method—Bread Machine—Time: 2½ hours

- Place ingredients into bread pan in order recommended by manufacturer.
- Select Dough and then press Start. Allow to mix, knead and rise.
- At end of Dough cycle, select Bake and then press Start. Bake 60-75 minutes.

No-Knead No-Rise Method—Bread Machine—Time: 1½ hours

- Add 1 tsp. baking soda and 1 Tbsp. baking powder to dry ingredients.
- Place ingredients into bread pan in order recommended by manufacturer.
- Select any mode that will mix the ingredients (i.e. Basic), then press Start.
- Mix the ingredients until well blended, 5-7 minutes, then press Stop.
- Select Bake and then press Start. There is no rise time. Bake 60-75 minutes.

For all methods, assist in mixing and make any necessary liquid adjustments.
For detailed bread machine instructions, see pages 125 through 129.

Oven Method

- You may bake all the recipes in this book in the oven. First, determine how you want to mix, knead and/or rise the ingredients. Then decide if you want the bread to rise before baking, or use the No-Knead No-Rise method.

For detailed oven instructions, see pages 130 through 132.

My Personalized Recipe for: ....

Date:________________ Baking method used:________________________

Amount and type of liquid used:____________________________________

Flours or mix used:____

Other changes:____

Notes:____

____

When personalizing with different flours or ingredients to suit your tastes, diet, for convenience, or for creativity, you may need to adjust the other ingredients.

My Personalized Recipe for: . . . .

Date:________________ Baking method used:_________________________

Amount and type of liquid used:______________________________________

Flours or mix used:____

Other changes:____

Notes:____

____

My Personalized Recipe for: . . . .

Date:________________ Baking method used:_________________________

Amount and type of liquid used:______________________________________

Flours or mix used:____

Other changes:____

Notes:____

____

My Personalized Recipe for: . . . .

Date:________________ Baking method used:_________________________

Amount and type of liquid used:______________________________________

Flours or mix used:____

Other changes:____

Notes:____

____

When personalizing with different flours or ingredients to suit your tastes, diet, for convenience, or for creativity, you may need to adjust the other ingredients.

Caribbean Sweet Bread

Pleasantly sweet and perfect for gift giving.

Wet Ingredients: (see page 6)

¾ cup	eggs
¾ cup	water, plus or minus
⅓ cup	sweetened condensed milk
1 teaspoon	vanilla extract
1 teaspoon	rice vinegar
2 Tablespoons	olive oil
½ teaspoon	lemon zest
3 Tablespoons	candied lemon and orange zest
¾ cup	raisins

Dry Ingredients: (see page 7)

1 cup	white rice flour
¾ cup	sweet potato starch
½ cup	tapioca starch flour
½ cup	cornstarch
¼ cup	yellow cornmeal

—or personalize with your favorite flour mix—

1 teaspoon	salt
¼ cup	sugar
¼ cup	dry milk powder
½ teaspoon	ground cloves
1 Tablespoon	xanthan gum
1 teaspoon	egg replacer
2½ teaspoons	yeast

Hint: *Use more sweetened condensed milk and less water for a sweeter taste and softer crust.*

How to candy zest: Remove the peel, without the white pith, from 2 lemons and 2 oranges. Bring 1 cup water and 1 cup of sugar to a boil. Add the peels and simmer until translucent. Remove from heat and let the zest cool in the syrup. Store in airtight container. To use in recipe, remove from the syrup and cut in pieces.

For Baking Methods, see pages 125-132.

Caribbean Picadillo: See "Beyond Bread," page 135.

Greek Olive and Feta Cheese Bread

"Perfect for a bruschetta bar. Consider it as a great substitute for pita bread to eat with Middle Eastern or Greek food, or with hummus."—Tanya

***Hint:** Canned black olives may be used instead of fresh Kalamata olives.*

Wet Ingredients: (see page 6)

¾ cup	eggs
¾ cup	water, plus or minus
1 teaspoon	cider vinegar
3 Tablespoons	olive oil
1 Tablespoon	light molasses
¼ cup	plain yogurt
¼ cup	diced red onions

Dry Ingredients: (see page 7)

1 cup	white rice flour
1 cup	brown rice flour
¼ cup	cornstarch
¼ cup	potato starch
½ cup	garfava (bean) flour

—or personalize with your favorite flour mix—

***FYI:** Kalamata olives have a rich, fruity flavor. Find them in jars and in grocery store olive bars. Rosemary is available fresh, dried or powdered. Use dried or powdered in this recipe.*

1 teaspoon	salt
¼ cup	dark brown sugar
½ cup	dry milk powder
1 Tablespoon	xanthan gum
½ teaspoon	white pepper
1 Tablespoon	dried Rosemary
2½ teaspoons	yeast

Add in:

¾ cup	feta cheese
½ cup	sliced Kalamata olives

Hummus spread: See "Beyond Bread," page 138.

Indian Curry and Honey Bread

Surprise your friends with this fantastic bread served as Curried Chicken Salad finger sandwiches.

Wet Ingredients: (see page 6)

¾ cup	eggs
¾ cup	buttermilk, plus or minus
1 teaspoon	vinegar
½ cup	unsalted butter, melted
¼ cup	honey
½ cup	coarsely chopped onion
½ cup	coarsely chopped tart apple

Hint: *No buttermilk on hand? Put the teaspoon of vinegar into a measuring cup. Add the ¾ cup of milk and allow to stand for five minutes. This will sour the milk.*

Dry Ingredients: (see page 7)

1 cup	white rice flour
¾ cup	brown rice flour
½ cup	tapioca starch flour
½ cup	potato starch
¼ cup	sorghum flour

—or personalize with your favorite flour mix—

1 teaspoon	salt
1 Tablespoon	xanthan gum
2 teaspoons	egg replacer
1 Tablespoon	sweet curry powder
2½ teaspoons	yeast

Add in:

¼ cup	shredded coconut
¼ cup	raisins
¼ cup	slivered almonds

FYI: *Curry powder is a blend of up to 20 different spices, herbs and seeds. The tastes of different brands of curry powders vary significantly. Read the blend of ingredients or try a couple of curries before deciding which brand you prefer.*

For
Baking Methods,
see pages 125-132.

Curried Chicken Salad Spread: See "Beyond Bread," page 136.

Italian Herb Bread

"I enjoyed this bread both topped with a grilled steak and onion, and as an accompaniment to warm chocolate."—Raquel

Wet Ingredients: (see page 6)

¾ cup	eggs
1 cup	milk, plus or minus
1 teaspoon	vinegar
¼ cup	olive oil

Dry Ingredients: (see page 7)

1 cup	white rice flour
1 cup	brown rice flour
½ cup	tapioca starch flour
½ cup	potato starch

—or personalize with your favorite flour mix—

2 Tablespoons	sweet rice flour
1 teaspoon	salt
3 Tablespoons	sugar
½ cup	dry milk powder
1 Tablespoon	xanthan gum
2½ teaspoons	yeast

Add in:

1 Tablespoon or more of dried Italian herbs

1 Tablespoon diced fresh garlic, or to taste

Hint: *Italian herbs can be a mixture of oregano, basil, marjoram, thyme and rosemary.*

Tip: *Milk gives the bread a softer crust. Use water for a crispier crust.*

How to dry your own herbs: *Microwave ¼ cup of fresh herbs on high for approximately 2 minutes. Keep dried and ground herbs in glass containers. The more airtight your container, the longer they will last.*

Crostini: Slice the bread thin, or use a cookie cutter for cutting bread circles. Brush with extra virgin olive oil, place on a cookie sheet and toast for approximately 5 minutes at 400°. Add toppings of your choice.

Bruschetta Spread: See "Beyond Bread," page 135.

For Baking Methods, see pages 125-132.

Mexican Salsa Bread

"I love the festive color, the smell and the great taste."–Raquel
"Excellent. Just a bit of a kick and a hint of cheese."–Sherry.

Wet Ingredients: (see page 6)

¾ cup	eggs
¼ cup	water, plus or minus
1 teaspoon	vinegar
1 Tablespoon	sunflower or vegetable oil
½ cup	salsa, mild or spicy

Hint: *If salsa is not available, use ½ cup of diced canned tomatoes.*

Dry Ingredients: (see page 7)

½ cup	white rice flour
½ cup	brown rice flour
½ cup	cornstarch
½ cup	sweet rice flour
1 cup	millet flour
¼ cup	amaranth flour

—or personalize with your favorite flour mix—

1 teaspoon	salt
1 Tablespoon	sugar
¼ cup	dry milk powder
1 Tablespoon	xanthan gum
2½ teaspoons	yeast

Tip: *When cutting hot peppers, wear plastic gloves or put a plastic bag on your hands so the juice does not get under your fingernails or onto your face.*

Add in:

2 Tablespoons	diced green chilies for a mild taste, or chopped jalapenos for a hotter taste
1 cup	shredded Mexican cheese combination such as Monterey Jack, Cheddar, Asadero and Queso Quesadilla or Manchego

Panettone Bread

For an impressive holiday presentation, cut the center out of the bread, fill with ice cream, and freeze until ready to serve.

Wet Ingredients: (see page 6)

¾ cup	eggs
½ cup	water, plus or minus
½ cup	sweetened condensed milk
1 teaspoon	rice vinegar
2 Tablespoons	unsalted butter, melted
1 Tablespoon	lemon zest

Dry Ingredients: (see page 7)

1 cup	white rice flour
½ cup	tapioca starch flour
¾ cup	potato starch
½ cup	cornstarch
¼ cup	sweet rice flour

—or personalize with your favorite flour mix—

1 teaspoon	salt
¼ cup	sugar
¼ cup	dry milk powder
1 teaspoon	egg replacer
1 Tablespoon	xanthan gum
2 teaspoons	anise seed
2½ teaspoons	yeast

Add in:

¼ cup	golden raisins
¼ cup	candied orange peel
¼ cup	chopped, dried apricots
¼ cup	dried cherries
2 Tablespoons	each of pine nuts and almonds

Tip: *Panettone is usually round. If possible, bake in a bread machine with a round pan, or cake tins.*

Hint: *Soak the dried cherries or dried apricots in brandy or fruit juice if hard.*

FYI: *See Caribbean Sweet Bread for instructions on how to make your own candied zest, or look for pre-made candied fruits, in gourmet sections of the grocery store.*

Portuguese Sweet Bread

One taste and you will know why it is recognized as one of the great traditional breads. It will remind you of many favorites.

Wet Ingredients: (see page 6)

¾ cup	eggs
¾ cup	water, plus or minus
½ cup	sweetened condensed milk
1 teaspoon	rice vinegar
2 Tablespoons	olive oil
½ teaspoon	grated lemon rind
1 teaspoon	vanilla extract

Dry Ingredients: (see page 7)

1 cup	white rice flour
½ cup	tapioca starch flour
½ cup	potato starch
½ cup	cornstarch
½ cup	sweet rice flour

—or personalize with your favorite flour mix—

1 teaspoon	salt
⅓ cup	sugar
¼ cup	dry milk powder
1 teaspoon	egg replacer
1 Tablespoon	xanthan gum
½ teaspoon	ground nutmeg (optional)
2½ teaspoons	yeast

***Hint:** If you do not have sweetened condensed milk, you can make a close substitute by blending together ½ cup powdered milk, ¼ cup sugar, 2 Tablespoons melted butter and 1 Tablespoon hot water in a blender until it is smooth.*

***FYI:** Sweetened condensed milk has water removed and sugar added, resulting in a sweet, thick, heavy syrup. It is not the same as evaporated milk, which is simply milk with 60% of the water taken out.*

"This makes fabulous French toast!"—Linda
"Reminded me of Italian Easter Bread."—Kathy

"Outstanding everything—taste, texture, moistness, versatility and overall usefulness. Reminds me of Hawaiian Sweet Bread or Pan de la Luce (Mexican Sweet Bread)."—Tanya

For Baking Methods, see pages 125-132.

Saffron Bread (Swedish)

"A wonderful New Years Eve treat when topped with a funky relish of grilled bell peppers and onions with balsamic vinegar and olive oil."—Tanya

Wet Ingredients: (see page 6)

¾ cup	eggs
¾ cup	milk, plus or minus
½ cup	unsalted butter, melted
1 teaspoon	vinegar
½ cup	currants or golden raisins

Dry Ingredients: (see page 7)

1 cup	white rice flour
1 cup	tapioca starch flour
1 cup	cornstarch
¼ cup	sweet rice flour

—or personalize with your favorite flour mix—

1 teaspoon	salt
⅓ cup	granulated sugar
½ cup	dry milk powder
1 Tablespoon	xanthan gum
2 teaspoons	egg replacer (optional)
2 teaspoons	saffron threads, toasted
2½ teaspoons	yeast

***FYI:** Saffron is known as the most expensive spice in the world.*

How to Toast Saffron Threads: Heat a dry skillet, then add 2 teaspoons of saffron threads. Continuously stir them with a spoon until the threads become slightly darker. Bring ½ cup of milk to a boil. Remove it from the heat and add the 2 teaspoons of toasted saffron thread. Allow to cool. When using the threads for the bread, strain them from the milk. Use the milk as part of the ¾ cup milk shown in the wet ingredients.

Santa Fe Blue Cornmeal Bread

"A complete surprise. It has so much flavor. Second only to the Reuben." –Kathy

Wet Ingredients: (see page 6)

3/4 cup	eggs
3/4 cup	milk, plus or minus
1 cup	plain or blueberry yogurt
1 teaspoon	vinegar

Dry Ingredients: (see page 7)

3/4 cup	white rice flour
3/4 cup	tapioca starch flour
3/4 cup	cornstarch
3/4 cup	blue cornmeal
1 teaspoon	salt
1/3 cup	sugar
1/2 cup	dry milk powder
2 teaspoons	egg replacer
1 Tablespoon	xanthan gum
2 1/2 teaspoons	yeast

Add in:

1 cup	fresh blueberries.

FYI: *There are three types of cornmeal; white, yellow and blue, depending on the type of corn.*

Hint: *If fresh blueberries are not available, use blueberry pie filling or frozen blueberries. You may need to adjust your liquid measurement by a tablespoon or more.*

Blue Cornmeal Chicken Beignet: See "Beyond Bread," page 135.

"This is the best cornbread I have ever had. Perfect with chili or topped with honey butter."–Tanya

For Baking Methods, see pages 125-132.

My Personalized Recipe for: ....

Date:________________ Baking method used:________________________

Amount and type of liquid used:________________________________

Flours or mix used:____

Other changes:____

Notes:____

____

My Personalized Recipe for: ....

Date:________________ Baking method used:________________________

Amount and type of liquid used:________________________________

Flours or mix used:____

Other changes:____

Notes:____

____

My Personalized Recipe for: ....

Date:________________ Baking method used:________________________

Amount and type of liquid used:________________________________

Flours or mix used:____

Other changes:____

Notes:____

____

When personalizing with different flours or ingredients to suit your tastes, diet, for convenience, or for creativity, you may need to adjust the other ingredients.

Very Vegetable Breads

Abbreviated Baking Methods

One Step Method—Bread Machine—Time: 3½ hours

- Place ingredients into bread pan in order recommended by manufacturer.
- Select Basic and then press Start.

Two Step Method—Bread Machine—Time: 2½ hours

- Place ingredients into bread pan in order recommended by manufacturer.
- Select Dough and then press Start. Allow to mix, knead and rise.
- At end of Dough cycle, select Bake and then press Start. Bake 60-75 minutes.

No-Knead No-Rise Method—Bread Machine—Time: 1½ hours

- Add 1 tsp. baking soda and 1 Tbsp. baking powder to dry ingredients.
- Place ingredients into bread pan in order recommended by manufacturer.
- Select any mode that will mix the ingredients (i.e. Basic), then press Start.
- Mix the ingredients until well blended, 5-7 minutes, then press Stop.
- Select Bake and then press Start. There is no rise time. Bake 60-75 minutes.

For all methods, assist in mixing and make any necessary liquid adjustments.
For detailed bread machine instructions, see pages 125 through 129.

Oven Method

- You may bake all the recipes in this book in the oven. First, determine how you want to mix, knead and/or rise the ingredients. Then decide if you want the bread to rise before baking, or use the No-Knead No-Rise method.

For detailed oven instructions, see pages 130 through 132.

My Personalized Recipe for: ....

Date:________________ Baking method used:________________________

Amount and type of liquid used:________________________________

Flours or mix used:______________________________________

Other changes:____

Notes:____

____

When personalizing with different flours or ingredients to suit your tastes, diet, for convenience, or for creativity, you may need to adjust the other ingredients.

My Personalized Recipe for: . . . .

Date:________________ Baking method used:________________________

Amount and type of liquid used:____________________________________

Flours or mix used:____

Other changes:____

Notes:____

____

My Personalized Recipe for: . . . .

Date:________________ Baking method used:________________________

Amount and type of liquid used:____________________________________

Flours or mix used:____

Other changes:____

Notes:____

____

My Personalized Recipe for: . . . .

Date:________________ Baking method used:________________________

Amount and type of liquid used:____________________________________

Flours or mix used:____

Other changes:____

Notes:____

____

When personalizing with different flours or ingredients to suit your tastes, diet, for convenience, or for creativity, you may need to adjust the other ingredients.

Black Bean Bread

"This hearty bread reminds me of Boston Brown bread."—Marie

Wet Ingredients: (see page 6)

3/4 cup	eggs
1/2 cup	water, plus or minus
1 teaspoon	red wine vinegar
1 Tablespoon	sesame oil
1 Tablespoon	canola oil
1 teaspoon	honey
1 clove	garlic, mashed

Dry Ingredients: (see page 7)

1 1/4 cup	brown rice flour
1/4 cup	sweet rice flour
1/4 cup	tapioca starch flour
1/4 cup	potato starch
1/4 cup	bean flour or quinoa flour
1/4 cup	buckwheat flour

—or personalize with your favorite flour mix—

1 teaspoon	salt
1 Tablespoon	brown sugar
1 Tablespoon	xanthan gum
1/2 teaspoon	dried oregano
1 teaspoon	curry powder
1/4 teaspoon	cayenne
1 teaspoon	caraway seeds
1 Tablespoon	orange zest
2 1/2 teaspoons	yeast

Add in:

1/2 cup	mashed, baked black beans

Curried Apricot Spread: See "Beyond Bread," page 136.

Hint: *Rinse and drain canned black beans before mashing.*

Tip: *Mild Mediterranean oregano is in most grocery stores. Mexican oregano has a stronger flavor and can be found in Latin markets or mail order.*

For Baking Methods, see pages 125-132.

Broccoli and Cheese Bread

"I enjoyed this bread. It has a great balance of flavors."—Bruce

Wet Ingredients: (see page 6)

3/4 cup	eggs
3/4 cup	water, plus or minus
1 teaspoon	rice vinegar
1/2 cup	gluten-free chicken broth

Dry Ingredients: (see page 7)

1 cup	white rice flour
1/2 cup	cornstarch
1/2 cup	tapioca starch flour
1/2 cup	sweet rice flour
1/2 cup	amaranth flour

—or personalize with your favorite flour mix—

1 teaspoon	salt
3 Tablespoons	sugar
1/2 cup	dry milk powder
2 teaspoons	xanthan gum
1 Tablespoon	egg replacer
2 1/2 teaspoons	yeast

Add in:

3/4 cup	steamed and chopped broccoli
1/2 cup	grated cheddar cheese

Hint: *There are gluten-free chicken bouillon cubes available on the market.*

Tip: *Keep refrigerated or frozen. This bread works best when allowed to rise before baking.*

FYI: *After you have opened a container of chicken broth, pour it into ice cube trays and freeze for when you need individual cubes for soup, in breads or other cooking adventures.*

Additional Bread Recipe:

Cauliflower and Cheese Bread:

- Instead of chicken broth, use 1/2 cup plain yogurt. Use steamed and chopped cauliflower instead of broccoli, and Swiss cheese instead of cheddar cheese.

Stuffed Mushroom: See "Beyond Bread," page 140.

Carrot Raisin Bread

A pretty, sunny looking bread with a pleasant, not too sweet taste.

Wet Ingredients: (see page 6)

¾ cup	eggs
¾ cup	water, plus or minus
1 teaspoon	vinegar
2 Tablespoons	vegetable oil
2 Tablespoons	honey
1 teaspoon	almond extract

Dry Ingredients: (see page 7)

¾ cup	white rice flour
¾ cup	brown rice flour
½ cup	tapioca starch flour
½ cup	potato starch
½ cup	bean flour
—or personalize with your favorite flour mix—	
2 Tablespoons	sweet rice flour
¼ cup	almond flour
1 teaspoon	salt
¼ cup	dry milk powder
1 Tablespoon	xanthan gum
1 Tablespoon	egg replacer
2 teaspoons	cinnamon
1 teaspoon	ground ginger
2½ teaspoons	yeast

***FYI:** Make your own almond flour. Grind together ½ cup blanched whole almonds and 1 Tablespoon of sugar. Pulse until it is a powder. Do not over pulse or it will turn into a paste—better for cookies than for bread.*

***Tip:** Usually the darker the honey, the stronger the flavor.*

Add in:

¾ cup loosely packed shredded carrots

⅓ cup raisins

***FYI:** Most honey used in the United States is in liquid form. Another form is whipped honey (also known as creamed honey or sugared honey). It is stored at room temperature and spread like butter.*

For Baking Methods, see pages 125-132.

Cinnamon Butter: See "Beyond Bread," page 136.

Garden Bread

"I feel healthy just eating this bread."–Bruce

Wet Ingredients: (see page 6)

¾ cup	eggs
⅓ cup	water, plus or minus
1 teaspoon	rice vinegar with basil
¼ cup	olive oil
⅓ cup	tomato juice

Hint: *Vegetables contain water and will add a "heaviness," as well as more liquid to the bread. The rise may be lower because of the ingredients.*

Dry Ingredients: (see page 7)

1 cup	white rice flour
1 cup	brown rice flour
¼ cup	tapioca starch flour
¼ cup	potato starch
½ cup	sweet rice flour

–or personalize with your favorite flour mix–

1 teaspoon	salt
¼ cup	light brown sugar
½ cup	dry milk powder
1 Tablespoon	xanthan gum
1 teaspoon	dried basil
1 teaspoon	celery seed
2½ teaspoons	yeast

Tip: *Cut the vegetables small. Otherwise they may cause the bread to fall apart.*

Add in:

½ cup	loosely packed, shredded carrots
2 Tablespoons	chopped green pepper
2 Tablespoons	sliced green onions
2 Tablespoons	raisins

For Baking Methods, see pages 125-132.

Recommendation: *This recipe works best when allowed to rise before baking.* ***FYI:*** *Keep refrigerated or frozen.*

Garden Sandwich: See "Beyond Bread," page 137.

Mushroom and Onion Bread

"I love the mushrooms in this bread. It is a perfect wrap for a mushroom potato salad." –Yvonne

Wet Ingredients: (see page 6)

¾ cup	eggs
¾ cup	water, plus or minus
1 teaspoon	vinegar
½ cup	unsalted butter, melted (1 stick)
2 Tablespoons	finely grated sweet onion
2 Tablespoons	light molasses

Dry Ingredients: (see page 7)

1 cup	white rice flour
1 cup	brown rice flour
½ cup	amaranth flour
½ cup	tapioca starch flour
—or personalize with your favorite flour mix—	
1 Tablespoon	buckwheat flour
1 teaspoon	salt
1 Tablespoon	mushroom powder
2 Tablespoons	dry milk powder
1 Tablespoon	xanthan gum
2½ teaspoons	yeast

Add In:

2 cups	cleaned, trimmed, finely chopped, loosely packed fresh mushrooms
1 ounce*	reconstituted, drained and finely chopped, dried mushrooms.

*Approximately 4-5

***Hint:** Make your own mushroom powder by grinding dried mushrooms to a fine powder. Mushroom powder may be used to flour fish or chicken.*

***Tip:** If using dried Shiitake mushrooms, remove the tough stems. Save for a soup stock or discard.*

***FYI:** Dry Shiitake mushrooms are high in trace minerals and B vitamins. The Porcini mushroom, also called Cepe has a nutty robust flavor.*

How to reconstitute dried mushrooms: Bring 1 cup of water to a boil. Add the dried mushrooms and remove the pot from the heat. Cover and let the mushrooms sit until soft, approximately 20-30 minutes. Drain, reserving the liquid for the water in this recipe.

Pumpkin Bread

"I love the looks of this bread and the crunchy seeds."—Sherry

Wet Ingredients: (see page 6)

¾ cup	eggs
¼ cup	water, plus or minus
1 teaspoon	cider vinegar
1 Tablespoon	pumpkin seed oil
¾ cup	sour cream
1 teaspoon	vanilla extract
1 cup	pure pumpkin, canned

Dry Ingredients: (see page 7)

1 cup	white rice flour
1 cup	sorghum flour
½ cup	sweet potato starch or cornstarch
½ cup	bean flour

—or personalize with your favorite flour mix—

1 teaspoon	salt
½ cup	light brown sugar
1 Tablespoon	xanthan gum
2 teaspoons	cinnamon
1 teaspoon	ground ginger
1 teaspoon	allspice
1 teaspoon	nutmeg
½ cup	pumpkin seeds
2½ teaspoons	yeast

Tip: *If you like spices add an extra ¼ to ½ teaspoons of chosen spices to the dry mixture. If you are not found of spices, cut back on the measurements shown.*

FYI: *Fresh pumpkin, goose-necked squash, acorn or butternut squash may be used. Bake thoroughly, cool, remove seeds and pulp. Beat the pulp until smooth with an electric mixer. This helps remove any strings as they will wind themselves around the mixer.*

Pumpkin Butter: See "Beyond Bread," page 140.

"Think of serving this with chili beans."—Nancy

Sun-Dried Tomato Garlic Bread

"Another all star home run."—Kathy

Wet Ingredients: (see page 6)

3/4 cup	eggs
1 cup	water, plus or minus
1 teaspoon	red wine vinegar
1/4 cup	olive oil
2 Tablespoons	cut up, reconstituted sun-dried tomatoes

Dry Ingredients: (see page 7)

1 cup	white rice flour
1 cup	brown rice flour
1/2 cup	tapioca starch flour
1/4 cup	amaranth flour
1/4 cup	soy flour

—or personalize with your favorite flour mix—

1 Tablespoon	sweet rice flour
1 teaspoon	salt
1/4 cup	brown sugar
1 Tablespoon	egg replacer
1 Tablespoon	xanthan gum
1 Tablespoon	Italian herbs
1 teaspoon	rosemary
1 teaspoon	garlic powder (not garlic salt)
2 1/2 teaspoons	yeast

Tip: *If no Italian herb mixture is on hand, use equal amounts of oregano, thyme and basil.*

FYI: *Sundried tomatoes can be found in health food stores and specialty sections of grocery stores. They are dried or in olive oil. If you are using the olive oil packed tomatoes, rinse completely before adding to the ingredients.*

"Use as hors devours with tomato, mozzarella and an olive on toasted bread cut into quarters."—Linda

For Baking Methods, see pages 125-132.

Sweet Potato with Pecans Bread

Warm this bread, then top with a handful of miniature marshmallows. Put under the broiler until the marshmallows brown and start to melt."–Denise

Hint: *The mashed sweet potatoes can be canned, fresh, baked, boiled or from Thanksgiving dinner.*

Wet Ingredients: (see page 6)

3/4 cup	eggs
3/4 cup	orange juice, plus or minus
2 Tablespoons	nut oil or vegetable oil
1 teaspoon	cider vinegar
1 teaspoon	vanilla extract
1 cup	mashed sweet potatoes

Dry Ingredients: (see page 7)

3/4 cup	white rice flour
3/4 cup	brown rice flour
1/2 cup	tapioca starch flour
1/2 cup	potato starch
1/2 cup	quinoa flour

—or personalize with your favorite flour mix—

2 Tablespoons	sweet rice flour
1 teaspoon	salt
1/4 cup	dark brown sugar
1/4 cup	dry milk powder
1 Tablespoon	xanthan gum
1 teaspoon	cinnamon
1/2 teaspoon	ground nutmeg
1/4 teaspoon	ground ginger
2 1/2 teaspoons	yeast

Tip: *This bread goes great with a ham and sweet potato casserole.*

Add in:

1/3 cup	raisins
1/3 cup	chopped pecans

For Baking Methods, see pages 125-132.

Triple Corn Bread

"Use roasted corn cut off the cob and roasted peppers for a smokier and deeper taste."—Marie

Wet Ingredients: (see page 6)

¾ cup	eggs
¾ cup	buttermilk, plus or minus
1 teaspoon	cider vinegar
1 Tablespoon	corn oil or sunflower oil
½ cup	cream style corn

Dry Ingredients: (see page 7)

¾ cup	white rice flour
¾ cup	brown rice flour
½ cup	tapioca starch flour
½ cup	cornstarch
¼ cup	corn flour
¼ cup	cornmeal

—or personalize with your favorite flour mix—

1 teaspoon	salt
1 Tablespoon	sugar
2 Tablespoons	dry milk powder
1 Tablespoon	xanthan gum
2½ teaspoons	yeast

Add in:

1 cup	drained whole kernel corn
½ cup	chopped red and green bell pepper

Hint: *If you do not have corn flour, use more cornmeal.*

FYI: *In the United States, corn flour and cornstarch are two separate things. Corn flour is from whole corn kernel ground into a fine flour, while corn-starch is from the endosperm part of the corn kernel.*

How to Roast Peppers: Cut the pepper in half and remove the seeds and cap. Squish the peppers so they are as flat as can be on a foil-lined cookie sheet, with the outside facing up. Broil. When most of the skin has blackened, remove from the oven and wrap in aluminum foil for 20 minutes to steam. Open the foil and peel the skin from the peppers. Slice into desired size.

My Personalized Recipe for: ....

Date:________________ Baking method used:____________________

Amount and type of liquid used:______________________________

Flours or mix used:____

Other changes:____

Notes:____

____

My Personalized Recipe for: ....

Date:________________ Baking method used:____________________

Amount and type of liquid used:______________________________

Flours or mix used:____

Other changes:____

Notes:____

____

My Personalized Recipe for: ....

Date:________________ Baking method used:____________________

Amount and type of liquid used:______________________________

Flours or mix used:____

Other changes:____

Notes:____

____

When personalizing with different flours or ingredients to suit your tastes, diet, for convenience, or for creativity, you may need to adjust the other ingredients.

Cheese, Nuts and Seed Breads

Abbreviated Baking Methods

One Step Method—Bread Machine—Time: 3½ hours

- Place ingredients into bread pan in order recommended by manufacturer.
- Select Basic and then press Start.

Two Step Method—Bread Machine—Time: 2½ hours

- Place ingredients into bread pan in order recommended by manufacturer.
- Select Dough and then press Start. Allow to mix, knead and rise.
- At end of Dough cycle, select Bake and then press Start. Bake 60-75 minutes.

No-Knead No-Rise Method—Bread Machine—Time: 1½ hours

- Add 1 tsp. baking soda and 1 Tbsp. baking powder to dry ingredients.
- Place ingredients into bread pan in order recommended by manufacturer.
- Select any mode that will mix the ingredients (i.e. Basic), then press Start.
- Mix the ingredients until well blended, 5-7 minutes, then press Stop.
- Select Bake and then press Start. There is no rise time. Bake 60-75 minutes.

For all methods, assist in mixing and make any necessary liquid adjustments.
For detailed bread machine instructions, see pages 125 through 129.

Oven Method

- You may bake all the recipes in this book in the oven. First, determine how you want to mix, knead and/or rise the ingredients. Then decide if you want the bread to rise before baking, or use the No-Knead No-Rise method.

For detailed oven instructions, see pages 130 through 132.

My Personalized Recipe for:. . . . .

Date:________________Baking method used:____________________________

Amount and type of liquid used:______________________________________

Flours or mix used:____

Other changes:____

Notes:____

____

When personalizing with different flours or ingredients to suit your tastes, diet, for convenience, or for creativity, you may need to adjust the other ingredients.

My Personalized Recipe for: ....

Date:________________ Baking method used:________________________

Amount and type of liquid used:________________________________

Flours or mix used:____

Other changes:____

Notes:____

____

My Personalized Recipe for: ....

Date:________________ Baking method used:________________________

Amount and type of liquid used:________________________________

Flours or mix used:____

Other changes:____

Notes:____

____

My Personalized Recipe for: ....

Date:________________ Baking method used:________________________

Amount and type of liquid used:________________________________

Flours or mix used:____

Other changes:____

Notes:____

____

When personalizing with different flours or ingredients to suit your tastes, diet, for convenience, or for creativity, you may need to adjust the other ingredients.

Bran and Flax Seed Bread

No one will suspect this bread is highly nutritious.

Wet Ingredients: (see page 6)

¾ cup	eggs
¼ cup	water, plus or minus
1 teaspoon	vinegar
½ cup	plain yogurt
1 cup	mashed bananas
1 Tablespoon	maple syrup or molasses

Dry Ingredients: (see page 7)

2 cups	white rice flour
½ cup	tapioca starch flour
½ cup	cornstarch or potato starch

—or personalize with your favorite flour mix—

1 teaspoon	salt
1 Tablespoon	dark brown sugar
½ cup	dry milk powder
½ cup	rice bran
1 Tablespoon	xanthan gum
1 teaspoon	cinnamon
2½ teaspoons	yeast

Add in:

¾ cup	dark raisins
½ cup	flax seed

***Hint:** Carrot juice, instead of water, will add vitamins and a richer color to your bread.*

***FYI:** Both dark and golden raisins are dried grapes. The dark raisins are ordinarily sun-dried, while the golden raisins are dried with artificial heat, resulting in a moister raisin.*

Grilled Bird and Beef Sandwich: See "Beyond Bread," page 137.

Artichoke Spread: See "Beyond Bread," page 135.

For Baking Methods, see pages 125-132.

Cheddar and Onion Bread

"This flavorful mild bread lends itself to spicy, tart, sweet and savory toppings. Whether you want a plain toast buttered, or a gourmet sandwich piled high with vegetables or meats, this bread is excellent as a base."—Marie

Wet Ingredients: (see page 6)

¾ cup	eggs
1 cup	water, plus or minus
1 teaspoon	cider vinegar
2 Tablespoons	vegetable oil
2 Tablespoons	honey

Hint: *If you do not have instant minced onions, use 1 Tablespoon or more of finely diced fresh sweet onion.*

Dry Ingredients: (see page 7)

1 cup	white rice flour
½ cup	tapioca starch flour
½ cup	cornstarch
¾ cup	quinoa flour
¼ cup	sweet rice flour

—or personalize with your favorite flour mix—

1 teaspoon	salt
½ cup	dry milk powder
2 teaspoons	xanthan gum
2 teaspoons	instant minced onions
2½ teaspoons	yeast

Tip: *Use a cookie cutter to cut shapes out of the bread. Top with whipped cream cheese and lightly sprinkle with paprika or grated sharp cheddar cheese.*

Add in:

1 cup	grated sharp cheddar cheese

Cheddar Cheese and Onion Sandwich: See "Beyond Bread," page 136.

Granola Bread

"This bread is a perfect candidate for meats–a meal or snack in itself–loved it!"–Raquel

Wet Ingredients: (see page 6)

3/4 cup	eggs
3/4 cup	apple juice, plus or minus
1 teaspoon	cider vinegar
2 Tablespoons	walnut or peanut oil
2 Tablespoons	honey
1 teaspoon	vanilla extract

Dry Ingredients: (see page 7)

1 cup	brown rice flour
1 cup	white rice flour
1/2 cup	tapioca starch flour
1/2 cup	potato starch

—or personalize with your favorite flour mix—

1 Tablespoon	flax seed meal
1 Tablespoon	almond meal
1 teaspoon	salt
1/2 cup	dry milk powder
1 Tablespoon	xanthan gum
2 1/2 teaspoons	yeast

Tip: *To save time, make extra granola nut and seed mixture. Store the unused mixture in the refrigerator, for when you make this bread again.*

Add in:

2 Tablespoons each of the following:

pine nuts
slivered almonds
shredded coconut
roughly chopped walnuts
shelled and unsalted pistachio nuts
shelled and unsalted pumpkin seeds
shelled and unsalted sunflower seeds
shelled and roughly chopped pecans

For Baking Methods, see pages 125-132.

Hannah's Healthy Bread

"Great meal companion. Loved the texture of the bread. Simply top with cream cheese–this bread is that good!"–Raquel

Wet Ingredients: (see page 6)

¾ cup	eggs
1¼ cups	water, plus or minus
1 teaspoon	vinegar
2 Tablespoons	oil
½ cup	applesauce
1 teaspoon	molasses
1 teaspoon	vanilla extract
1 teaspoon	flax seed meal

Dry Ingredients: (see page 7)

1 cup	white rice flour
1 cup	brown rice flour
⅓ cup	tapioca starch flour
⅓ cup	potato starch
⅓ cup	garfava bean flour

—or personalize with your favorite flour mix—

1 Tablespoon	flax seed
2 Tablespoons	buckwheat flour
1 teaspoon	salt
2 Tablespoons	dark brown sugar
1 Tablespoon	xanthan gum
2½ teaspoons	yeast

Add in:

2 Tablespoons	chopped walnuts

Hint: *Due to the heartiness of the bread, this recipe can take longer to bake.*

Tip: *Flax seed is a great source of Omega-3 fatty acids. You can find them in health food stores, some grocery stores and mail order.*

FYI: *Keep refrigerated or frozen. This recipe works best when allowed to rise before baking.*

For Sandwich Suggestions, see "Beyond Bread," page 133.

Hazelnut and Cranberries Bread

A festive, tasteful bread that makes a beautiful presentation.

Wet Ingredients: (see page 6)

¾ cup	eggs
½ cup	water, plus or minus
½ cup	berry or plain yogurt
1 teaspoon	red wine vinegar
¼ cup	maple syrup
1 teaspoon	hazelnut extract

Dry Ingredients: (see page 7)

1 cup	white rice flour
½ cup	cornstarch
½ cup	tapioca starch flour
½ cup	potato starch
½ cup	sorghum flour

—or personalize with your favorite flour mix—

1 teaspoon	salt
1 Tablespoon	sugar
2 Tablespoons	dry milk powder
1 teaspoon	egg replacer
1 Tablespoon	xanthan gum
2½ teaspoons	yeast

Add in:

¾ cup	coarsely chopped toasted hazelnuts
½ cup	fresh cranberries, halved

Hint: *Frozen cranberries, canned cranberries or dried cranberries may also be used. You will need to adjust the liquids accordingly.*

Tip: *Hazelnuts are also called filberts or cobnuts.*

How to Toast Hazelnuts: The skin of the hazelnut is bitter and should be removed. Toasting brings out the flavor of the nuts. Toast the nuts by baking them on a cookie sheet at 400° for about 5 minutes or the skin starts to flake away from the nut. While warm, rub the nuts together in a dish towel to remove as much skin as possible. Or, look for pre-peeled and toasted hazelnuts in specialty food stores.

For
Baking Methods,
see pages 125-132.

Peanuts and (Un)Cola Bread

"Surprisingly good! Top with jelly. I liked this bread the best."—Vicenta

Wet Ingredients: (see page 6)

¾ cup	eggs
1 cup	uncola or cola, plus or minus
1 Tablespoon	vegetable oil

***Hint:** If unsalted peanuts are not available, remove the majority of the salt by rubbing them in a towel or by shaking salted peanuts in a colander.*

Dry Ingredients: (see page 7)

1 cup	white rice flour
1 cup	sweet rice flour
1 cup	quinoa flour

—or personalize with your favorite flour mix—

1 teaspoon	salt
3 Tablespoons	light brown sugar
¼ cup	dry milk powder
1 Tablespoon	xanthan gum
2½ teaspoons	yeast

Add in:

½ cup	sharp cheddar cheese
¾ cup	shelled, crushed unsalted peanuts

***Tip:** Substitute cashews for a different taste.*

"I liked the peanut chunks in the bread."—Ron
"I would serve it with Chinese food."—Jan

***FYI:** Different varieties of peanuts are available, like honey-peanuts or spiced peanuts. Verify they are wheat gluten-free.*

Honey Grilled Cheese: See "Beyond Bread," page 138.

For Baking Methods, see pages 125-132.

Seed Bread

"I could hardly keep from eating the entire loaf in one sitting." —Marie

Wet Ingredients: (see page 6)

¾ cup	eggs
1 cup	water, plus or minus
3 Tablespoons	oil
1 teaspoon	vinegar
2 Tablespoons	honey

Tip: *Refrigerate or freeze seeds and nuts in an airtight container to prevent them from turning rancid.*

Dry Ingredients: (see page 7)

1 cup	white rice flour
¾ cup	brown rice flour
½ cup	tapioca starch flour
½ cup	cornstarch
2 Tablespoons	sweet rice flour
2 Tablespoons	buckwheat flour

—or personalize with your favorite flour mix—

1 teaspoon	salt
½ cup	dry milk powder
1 Tablespoon	xanthan gum
2½ teaspoons	yeast

Hint: *Make enough seed mixture for two or three breads. Add some raisins to the leftover seed mixture and put it on top of your cereal in the morning or sprinkle on salads.*

Add in:

A mixture of ¼ cup each: shelled sunflower seeds, pumpkin seeds and sesame seeds.

1 Tablespoon	poppy seeds
2 teaspoons	flax seeds
½ teaspoon	anise seeds

Green Onion Scramble: See "Beyond Bread," page 137.

"I couldn't wait to make this bread. If I didn't like it, I thought, the birds would love me for it. Well, I love it! Sorry birds" —Kitten

Wild Rice Bread

"I love this bread with soup, or simply topped with peanut butter or with turkey, cranberries, and cream cheese. During the summer, bread and butter pickles atop mayonnaise gives this bread a great, out of the ordinary crunch."–Marie

Wet Ingredients: (see page 6)

¾ cup	eggs
1¼ cup	water, plus or minus
1 teaspoon	cider vinegar
3 Tablespoons	oil
¾ cup	cooked, drained, cooled wild rice

Dry Ingredients: (see page 7)

1 cup	white rice flour
¾ cup	brown rice flour
½ cup	tapioca starch flour
½ cup	cornstarch
¼ cup	buckwheat flour

—or personalize with your favorite flour mix—

1 teaspoon	salt
2 Tablespoons	brown sugar
1 teaspoon	white pepper
½ cup	dry milk powder
2 teaspoons	xanthan gum
2½ teaspoons	yeast

Tip: *Wild rice cooking time*
Black 45-60 min.
Brown 30-45 min.
Blonde 10-20 min.
Instant 3-10 min.

Hint: *1 cup uncooked wild rice yields 3-4 cups cooked*

How to cook wild rice: Simmer wild rice in three parts water or broth to one part rice until it is done. Water should cover the rice. Wild rice is done when most of the kernels are split open. You will be able to see the white inside. It will be tender, but still a little chewy.

Cranberry Sandwich Spread: See "Beyond Bread," page 136.

For
Baking Methods,
see pages 125-132.

Savory to Sweet Fruit Breads

Morning Glory Bread 105

The test of a truly great gluten-free bread is if it can stand up on its own–without embellishments, toppings or toasting. Our taste testers all agree this bread fits those criteria.

Peach Apricot Bread 106

A "peachy-colored" breakfast bread. It is equally as good as a mid-afternoon snack with lemon curd or peach preserves and a cup of tea. As a dessert, simply warm it and top with vanilla ice cream.

Peaches and Almond Bread 107

Pear Hazelnut Bread 107

A great snack or tea bread. The pears provide a pleasing delicate taste, particularly when balanced with the hazelnut meal. A special bread for mild flavored fillings, such as a turkey sandwich.

Plum, Lemon, Orange Bread 108

It sounds so nutritious, slightly sweet and interesting. Envision it with milk goat cheese, or thinly sliced mozzarella cheese and a jar of apricot jam.

Abbreviated Baking Methods

One Step Method—Bread Machine—Time: 3½ hours

- Place ingredients into bread pan in order recommended by manufacturer.
- Select Basic and then press Start.

Two Step Method—Bread Machine—Time: 2½ hours

- Place ingredients into bread pan in order recommended by manufacturer.
- Select Dough and then press Start. Allow to mix, knead and rise.
- At end of Dough cycle, select Bake and then press Start. Bake 60-75 minutes.

No-Knead No-Rise Method—Bread Machine—Time: 1½ hours

- Add 1 tsp. baking soda and 1 Tbsp. baking powder to dry ingredients.
- Place ingredients into bread pan in order recommended by manufacturer.
- Select any mode that will mix the ingredients (i.e. Basic), then press Start.
- Mix the ingredients until well blended, 5-7 minutes, then press Stop.
- Select Bake and then press Start. There is no rise time. Bake 60-75 minutes.

For all methods, assist in mixing and make any necessary liquid adjustments.
For detailed bread machine instructions, see pages 125 through 129.

Oven Method

- You may bake all the recipes in this book in the oven. First, determine how you want to mix, knead and/or rise the ingredients. Then decide if you want the bread to rise before baking, or use the No-Knead No-Rise method.

For detailed oven instructions, see pages 130 through 132.

My Personalized Recipe for: . . . .

Date:________________ Baking method used:______________________

Amount and type of liquid used:______________________________

Flours or mix used:_______________________________________

Other changes:____

Notes:____

____

When personalizing with different flours or ingredients to suit your tastes, diet, for convenience, or for creativity, you may need to adjust the other ingredients.

My Personalized Recipe for: ....

Date: ________________ Baking method used: ________________________

Amount and type of liquid used: ________________________________

Flours or mix used: ____

Other changes: ____

Notes: ____

____

My Personalized Recipe for: ....

Date: ________________ Baking method used: ________________________

Amount and type of liquid used: ________________________________

Flours or mix used: ____

Other changes: ____

Notes: ____

____

My Personalized Recipe for: ....

Date: ________________ Baking method used: ________________________

Amount and type of liquid used: ________________________________

Flours or mix used: ____

Other changes: ____

Notes: ____

____

When personalizing with different flours or ingredients to suit your tastes, diet, for convenience, or for creativity, you may need to adjust the other ingredients.

Apricot and Almonds Bread

The sweetness of the bread requires very little in the line of a topping.–Marie

Wet Ingredients: (see page 6)

¾ cup	eggs
¾ cup	apricot nectar juice, plus or minus
1 teaspoon	cider vinegar
2 teaspoons	vegetable oil
2 Tablespoons	honey

Dry Ingredients: (see page 7)

1 cup	white rice flour
½ cup	brown rice flour
½ cup	tapioca starch flour
½ cup	quinoa flour
½ cup	garfava bean flour

–or personalize with your favorite flour mix–

1 teaspoon	salt
1 Tablespoon	light brown sugar
⅓ cup	dry milk powder
1 Tablespoon	xanthan gum
½ teaspoon	allspice or cinnamon
¼ teaspoon	nutmeg
2½ teaspoons	yeast

Tip: *Allspice tastes like a combination of nutmeg, cinnamon and cloves.*

Add in:

¾ cup	sliced reconstituted dried apricots
½ cup	toasted almond slivers

How to Reconstitute Dried Apricots: Soak for 10 minutes in ¼ cup hot water. Drain and allow to cool.

"This is an awesome bread."–Kathy

For Baking Methods, see pages 125-132.

Date, Cumin and Coriander Bread

"One of our favorite breads. You may have to stop yourself from eating the entire loaf in one sitting." –Marie

Hint: *Warm any leftover date puree as a bread topping along with whipped cream. The pureed date mixture is also irresistible as a salad dressing.*

FYI: *Dates are a good source of protein and iron.*

Wet Ingredients: (see page 6)

¾ cup	eggs
¾ cup	water, plus or minus
¼ cup	apple juice
¾ cup	pureed date mixture from preparation step below

Dry Ingredients: (see page 7)

1 cup	white rice flour
½ cup	brown rice flour
½ cup	tapioca starch flour
½ cup	potato starch
½ cup	sweet rice flour

—or personalize with your favorite flour mix—

1 teaspoon	salt
¼ cup	light brown sugar
1 Tablespoon	xanthan gum
2½ teaspoons	yeast

Preparation for pureed date mixture:

Finely chop 16 dates (about 4 oz).
Boil them in ½ cup water for 2 minutes.
Remove from heat, cover, let stand 1 hour to soften.
Transfer date mixture to a blender.

Add:

½ cup	fresh lime juice
3 Tablespoons	olive oil
1 Tablespoon	dried oregano
2 teaspoons	honey
2 teaspoons	ground cumin
2 teaspoons	ground coriander

Puree until smooth.

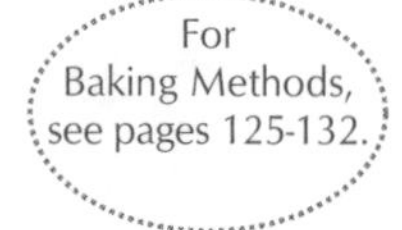
For
Baking Methods,
see pages 125-132.

Date Nut Bread

"I enjoyed eating this on its own, without toppings." –Russ

Wet Ingredients: (see page 6)

3/4 cup	eggs
1/4 cup	water, plus or minus
1 teaspoon	vanilla extract
1/4 cup	olive oil
3/4 cup	apple juice

Dry Ingredients: (see page 7)

1 cup	white rice flour
1/2 cup	brown rice flour
1/2 cup	tapioca starch flour or cornstarch
1/2 cup	potato starch
1/2 cup	sweet rice flour

–or personalize with your favorite flour mix–

1 teaspoon	salt
1/4 cup	sugar
1 Tablespoon	xanthan gum
2 1/2 teaspoons	yeast

Add in:

3/4 cup	chopped dates
1 cup	chopped walnuts

***Hint:** Use applesauce instead of the oil for a sweeter bread.*

***FYI:** "This recipe works well using the No-Knead No-Rise Method. It has the rise of a yeast bread and the moistness and density of a quick bread." –LynnRae*

"Date Nut Bread ranks right up there with rye and pizza breads." –Denise

"Excellent, so moist even after a few days. Great plain as a snack." –Kathy

Figs, Orange and Almond Bread

"I thoroughly enjoyed this bread. The name didn't entice me, but the aroma, texture and taste certainly did!" –Vicki

Hint: *Use a scissor sprayed with olive oil to snip the dried figs into fourths or sixths.*

Wet Ingredients: (see page 6)

¾ cup	eggs
¾ cup	water, plus or minus
1 teaspoon	lemon juice
1 Tablespoon	walnut oil
⅓ cup	sour cream
⅓ cup	orange marmalade
½ teaspoon	almond extract

Dry Ingredients: (see page 7)

1 cup	white rice flour
½ cup	brown rice flour
½ cup	tapioca starch flour
½ cup	potato starch
½ cup	sweet rice flour

—or personalize with your favorite flour mix—

Tip: *Look for gluten-free fig jam in specialty food stores. Use ½ cup fig jam instead of the snipped dried figs.*

1 teaspoon	salt
¼ cup	light brown sugar
1 Tablespoon	xanthan gum
2½ teaspoons	yeast

Add in:

1 cup	snipped dried figs
1 cup	slivered almonds

FYI: *Figs were once considered a sacred fruit and a symbol of peace and prosperity.*

The difference between a jelly and a jam: In jelly, the fruit comes in the form of fruit juice. In jam, the fruit comes in the form of fruit pulp or crushed fruit. Both are suitable for these bread recipes. In preserves or marmalade, the fruit comes in the form of chunks in a syrup or a jam and must be strained. The larger pieces of fruit may then be diced to be included in the bread.

Green Olive Bread

Funky and fun, this bread makes great toast and sandwich. We particularly enjoyed it for appetizers and quick snacks.

Wet Ingredients: (see page 6)

¾ cup	eggs
1 teaspoon	cider vinegar
2 Tablespoons	olive oil
¾ cup	water, plus or minus
2 Tablespoons	pimentos

Dry Ingredients: (see page 7)

¾ cup	white rice flour
1 cup	brown rice flour
¼ cup	cornstarch
¼ cup	potato starch flour
½ cup	cornmeal
¼ cup	millet flour

—or personalize with your favorite flour mix—

1 teaspoon	salt
¼ cup	sugar
½ cup	dry milk powder
1 Tablespoon	dried basil
1 Tablespoon	xanthan gum
2½ teaspoon	yeast

Add in:

½ cup	chopped green olives

***Hint:** Green olives are available stuffed with pimentos, almonds, jalapenos, pickles and more.*

***Tip:** Add 1 cup of Parmesan cheese for a totally different bread flavor.*

Pimento Cheese Spread: See "Beyond Bread," page 139.

Tofu Spread: See "Beyond Bread," page 141.

For Baking Methods, see pages 125-132.

Lemon Poppy Seed Bread

"The grand kids thought this bread was great! They loved the pop of the poppy seeds and the zing of the lemon."—Charlene

Hint: *Use lemon olive oil (available in specialty stores) for added zip.*

Wet Ingredients: (see page 6)

¾ cup	eggs
¾ cup	water, plus or minus
2 teaspoons	lemon juice
2 Tablespoons	oil
½ cup	lemon yogurt
1 teaspoon	almond extract
1 teaspoon	lemon zest

Dry Ingredients: (see page 7)

1½ cups	white rice flour
¼ cup	potato starch
½ cup	tapioca starch flour
¼ cup	cornstarch
¼ cup	sweet rice flour
½ cup	millet flour

—or personalize with your favorite flour mix—

1 teaspoon	salt
3 Tablespoons	sugar
½ cup	dry milk powder
1 Tablespoon	xanthan gum
2 teaspoons	egg replacer
2 Tablespoons	poppy seeds
2½ teaspoons	yeast

Tip: *If using a thick sour cream instead of a thin lemon yogurt, you may need to add more water.*

Lemon Icing: See "Beyond Bread," page 138.

For
Baking Methods,
see pages 125-132.

Morning Glory Bread

Morning glory bread is equally good, whether served cold or warm.–Denise

Wet Ingredients: (see page 6)

¾ cup	eggs
½ cup	water, plus or minus
1 teaspoon	red wine vinegar
½ cup	applesauce
2 Tablespoons	honey
2 teaspoons	vanilla extract
2 Tablespoons	freshly grated apple

Dry Ingredients: (see page 7)

¾ cup	white rice flour
¾ cup	brown rice flour
½ cup	tapioca starch flour
½ cup	potato starch
¼ cup	millet flour
2 Tablespoons	sweet rice flour
2 Tablespoons	rice bran

—or personalize with your favorite flour mix—

1 teaspoon	salt
1 Tablespoon	xanthan gum
1 teaspoon	cinnamon
2½ teaspoons	yeast

Add in:

¼ cup	drained pineapple bits, cut into quarters
½ cup	loosely packed grated carrots
¼ cup	raisins
¼ cup	finely chopped walnuts

FYI: *Keep refrigerated or frozen. This recipe works best when allowed to rise before baking. Use the No-Knead No-Rise Method if you want a moist cake-type bread and allow to bake 10 minutes longer.*

Hint: *Make this recipe with the recommended fruit and vegetables. Increasing should be done ¼ cup at a time, otherwise the bread will become too heavy and will take too long to bake.*

Tip: *Make this bread into muffins. They are healthy and hearty for on-the-road trips, a snack at the office or over a leisurely cup of coffee.*

Peach Apricot Bread

"Dress up this bread with powdered sugar sprinkled on top." –Raquel

Wet Ingredients: (see page 6)

¾ cup	eggs
¾ cup	peach juice, plus or minus
2 Tablespoons	oil
½ cup	peach yogurt
1 teaspoon	vanilla extract

Dry Ingredients: (see page 7)

2 cups	white rice flour
½ cup	tapioca starch flour
½ cup	cornstarch

—or personalize with your favorite flour mix—

1 teaspoon	salt
2 Tablespoons	brown sugar
¼ cup	dry milk powder
1 Tablespoon	xanthan gum
½ teaspoon	nutmeg
1 teaspoon	cinnamon
2½ teaspoons	yeast

Add in:

½ cup	chopped dried peaches
¼ cup	chopped dried apricots

Hint: *Fresh fruit or drained canned peaches may also be used. Because they will be moister, cut back on the liquid by a tablespoon or more. Use the juice from the can as part of your liquid.*

Tip: *Peach juice can be found in the juice section of most stores.*

"The next time I make this, I will put in twice the amount of dried fruit." –Denise

"I am not a nutmeg enthusiast, so I would skip the nutmeg in this recipe." –Sherry

For Baking Methods, see pages 125-132.

Pear Hazelnut Bread

Fruit-filled with complex flavors–add macadamia nuts as part of your nut mixture.

Wet Ingredients: (see page 6)

¾ cup	eggs
¾ cup	pear juice, plus or minus
1 teaspoon	vinegar
¼ cup	strained apricot preserves
1 teaspoon	hazelnut extract
1 teaspoon	pure almond extract
3 ripe pears	washed, skinned and cut into small pieces

***Hint:** Strain the preserves to remove any major pieces of apricots. Use the strained part for the dough, If desired, cut up the apricot pieces into small sizes and add to dough. Or use as a topping.*

Dry Ingredients: (see page 7)

1 cup	white rice flour
½ cup	brown rice flour
½ cup	tapioca starch flour
½ cup	cornstarch
½ cup	potato starch

–or personalize with your favorite flour mix–

½ cup	hazelnut meal
1 teaspoon	salt
1 Tablespoon	sugar
3 teaspoons	egg replacer
1 Tablespoon	xanthan gum
2½ teaspoons	yeast

How to make Nut Meal Flour: Grind toasted hazelnuts in food processor with 1 Tablespoon sugar until flour-like or becomes a meal.

Additional Bread Recipe:

Peaches and Almond Bread:

- Use fresh peaches instead of fresh pears.
- Substitute peach jam for apricot preserves and almond flour for hazelnut flour.
- Double the amount of almond extract and omit the hazelnut extract.

Plum, Lemon and Orange Bread

Slightly toasted, the features of this bread come to life.

Wet Ingredients: (see page 6)

¾ cup	eggs
⅓ cup	orange marmalade
⅓ cup	lemon or plain yogurt
¼ cup	water, plus or minus
¼ cup	prune juice or puree
2 teaspoons	lemon juice
1 teaspoon	vanilla extract
1 teaspoon	lemon zest

Dry Ingredients: (see page 7)

1 cup	white rice flour
½ cup	brown rice flour
½ cup	tapioca starch flour
½ cup	potato starch or cornstarch
½ cup	sweet rice flour

—or personalize with your favorite flour mix—

1 teaspoon	salt
¼ cup	brown sugar
1 Tablespoon	xanthan gum
2½ teaspoons	yeast

Add in:

¾ cup	chopped, dried plums (prunes)
½ cup	toasted sesame seeds

***Hint:** A prune is a dried plum. The popular name these days is dried plum, not prune.*

***Tip:** Plums are also available canned.*

This is a great tea bread. Serve as finger sandwiches for a party, or toast small pieces for a snack instead of chips. Combine orange marmalade with cream cheese for an easy topping. Thinly sliced turkey is a welcome addition. Or whip cream cheese with lemon peel and a touch of lemon extract. Serve with hot apple cider.

Dawn to Dusk Delectable Breads

Very Berry & Marshmallow Bread . . . 119

This beautifully colored bread is for the kids–and the kid in all of us. They love how it is sweet, lightly, sticky and squishy–due to the fruit and marshmallows. For a less sticky bread, leave out the marshmallows.

White Chocolate and Almond Bread . . 120

Add something special to your late night snack. This moist bread with sweet pockets of white chocolate is delicious when topped with strawberries and créme fraiche.

Zucchini Blueberry Bread 121

Zucchini and Blueberries, oh my! Enjoy your fruit and veggies in this fun bread. The ingredients compliment each other in every morsel.

Zucchini Chocolate Blueberry Bread 121

Abbreviated Baking Methods

One Step Method—Bread Machine—Time: 3½ hours

- Place ingredients into bread pan in order recommended by manufacturer.
- Select Basic and then press Start.

Two Step Method—Bread Machine—Time: 2½ hours

- Place ingredients into bread pan in order recommended by manufacturer.
- Select Dough and then press Start. Allow to mix, knead and rise.
- At end of Dough cycle, select Bake and then press Start. Bake 60-75 minutes.

No-Knead No-Rise Method—Bread Machine—Time: 1½ hours

- Add 1 tsp. baking soda and 1 Tbsp. baking powder to dry ingredients.
- Place ingredients into bread pan in order recommended by manufacturer.
- Select any mode that will mix the ingredients (i.e. Basic), then press Start.
- Mix the ingredients until well blended, 5-7 minutes, then press Stop.
- Select Bake and then press Start. There is no rise time. Bake 60-75 minutes.

For all methods, assist in mixing and make any necessary liquid adjustments.
For detailed bread machine instructions, see pages 125 through 129.

Oven Method

- You may bake all the recipes in this book in the oven. First, determine how you want to mix, knead and/or rise the ingredients. Then decide if you want the bread to rise before baking, or use the No-Knead No-Rise method.

For detailed oven instructions, see pages 130 through 132.

My Personalized Recipe for: . . . .

Date:________________ Baking method used:________________________

Amount and type of liquid used:______________________________

Flours or mix used:_______________________________________

Other changes:____

Notes:____

____

When personalizing with different flours or ingredients to suit your tastes, diet, for convenience, or for creativity, you may need to adjust the other ingredients.

My Personalized Recipe for:

Date: ____________ Baking method used: ____________

Amount and type of liquid used: ____________

Flours or mix used: ____________

Other changes: ____________

Notes: ____________

My Personalized Recipe for:

Date: ____________ Baking method used: ____________

Amount and type of liquid used: ____________

Flours or mix used: ____________

Other changes: ____________

Notes: ____________

My Personalized Recipe for:

Date: ____________ Baking method used: ____________

Amount and type of liquid used: ____________

Flours or mix used: ____________

Other changes: ____________

Notes: ____________

When personalizing with different flours or ingredients to suit your tastes, diet, for convenience, or for creativity, you may need to adjust the other ingredients.

Chocolate Cherry Bread

"One of my favorite dessert breads. Try it without the cherries and add more chocolate instead. It is wonderful."–Bruce

Wet Ingredients: (see page 6)

3/4 cup	eggs
3/4 cup	buttermilk, plus or minus
1 teaspoon	red wine vinegar
1/4 cup	unsalted butter, melted

Dry Ingredients: (see page 7)

1 1/2 cups	white rice flour
1/2 cup	brown rice flour
1/2 cup	tapioca starch flour
1/2 cup	cornstarch

—or personalize with your favorite flour mix—

1 teaspoon	salt
1/4 cup	sugar
1/2 cup	dry milk powder
2 Tablespoons	cocoa powder
1 Tablespoon	xanthan gum
2 1/2 teaspoons	yeast

Add in:

1/2 cup	dried cherries soaked in 1/4 cup rum or water

***Hint:** Drain cherries before adding to bread mixture, unless you include the rum as part of the liquid measurement.*

***Tip:** For an adult dessert, top with a cherry liqueur.*

***FYI:** We used frozen cherries, fresh cherries, cherries in a can, dried cherries, maraschino cherries and cherry pie filling. They all worked splendidly. The liquid ingredients needed to be adjusted accordingly.*

For Baking Methods, see pages 125-132.

Chocolate Hazelnut Spread: See "Beyond Bread," page 136.

Ginger Bread

"Great toasted with butter, cinnamon and sugar sprinkled on top."—Debbie

Wet Ingredients: (see page 6)

¾ cup	eggs
1¼ cup	milk, plus or minus
3 Tablespoons	unsalted butter, melted
1 teaspoon	vinegar
¼ cup	dark corn syrup

Dry Ingredients: (see page 7)

1 cup	white rice flour
1 cup	brown rice flour
¼ cup	cornstarch
¼ cup	tapioca starch flour
¼ cup	potato starch
¼ cup	millet flour

—or personalize with your favorite flour mix—

1 teaspoon	salt
¼ cup	light brown sugar
1 Tablespoon	xanthan gum
2 Tablespoons	egg replacer
1 Tablespoon	ground ginger
2 teaspoons	ground cinnamon
¼ teaspoon	grated nutmeg
¼ teaspoon	ground cloves
1 teaspoon	rye flavor (optional)
2½ teaspoons	yeast

"A simple topping is whipped cream sweetened with vanilla and confectioners sugar."—Doug

"Fabulous as French toast. You have to try it!" —Bruce and LynnRae

Gingered Ginger Bread

"Absolutely wonderful when warmed."—Marie

Wet Ingredients: (see page 6)

¾ cup	eggs
1¼ cups	milk, plus or minus
3 Tablespoons	unsalted butter, melted
1 teaspoon	vinegar
¼ cup	light molasses
¼ cup	finely grated fresh ginger root

Dry Ingredients: (see page 7)

1 cup	white rice flour
1 cup	brown rice flour
¼ cup	cornstarch
¼ cup	tapioca starch flour
¼ cup	potato starch
¼ cup	quinoa flour

—or personalize with your favorite flour mix—

1 teaspoon	salt
¼ cup	dark brown sugar
1 Tablespoon	xanthan gum
2 Tablespoons	egg replacer
2 Tablespoons	finely chopped crystallized ginger
1 teaspoon	dried ground ginger
1 teaspoon	rye flavor (optional)
2½ teaspoons	yeast

***Hint:** Fresh ginger is in the grocery store vegetable department. You can purchase a "hand'"of ginger root or just break off the length you want. Look for pieces that have a smooth outer skin.*

***Tip:** Crystallized ginger has been cooked and covered with sugar. It is also known as candied ginger and may be found in the grocery store baking department.*

***FYI:** You can freeze unpeeled fresh ginger for a couple of months.*

For Baking Methods, see pages 125-132.

Holiday Fruit Bread

"A duo recipe! For a wonderful basic bread omit the walnuts and candied fruit. An easy recipe to use in the oven as rolls or baguettes."–Charlene

Wet Ingredients: (see page 6)

¾ cup	eggs
½ cup	water
1 cup	milk, plus or minus
2 Tablespoons	oil
1 teaspoon	vanilla extract

Dry Ingredients: (see page 7)

2 cups	white rice flour
½ cup	sweet rice flour
½ cup	tapioca starch flour
½ cup	potato starch

—or personalize with your favorite flour mix—

2 teaspoons	salt
¼ cup	sugar
1 teaspoon	egg replacer
1 Tablespoon	xanthan gum
2½ teaspoons	yeast

Add in:

½ cup	walnuts
¾ cup	candied fruit

***Hint:** A dried fruit mixture such as dates, raisins and pineapple is a great substitute for candied fruit.*

***Tip:** You may also use fruit cocktail from the can. Remember to adjust the liquid ingredients since canned fruit carries a lot of liquid. Cut the fruit pieces small, or they will tend to make the bread fall apart.*

For Baking Methods, see pages 125-132.

Lemon Orange Glaze: See "Beyond Bread," page 138.

Thanks Charlene, for contributing this wonderful recipe for all to enjoy.

Macadamia Pineapple Bread

"Putting any kind of topping on Macadamia Pineapple Bread would be a shame. It is great as is." –Toni and Linda

Wet Ingredients: (see page 6)

¾ cup	eggs
¼ cup	water, plus or minus
¾ cup	pineapple juice
3 Tablespoons	macadamia nut oil

Dry Ingredients: (see page 7)

1 cup	white rice flour
1 cup	brown rice flour
½ cup	cornstarch
½ cup	potato starch
—or personalize with your favorite flour mix—	
2 Tablespoons	sweet rice flour
½ cup	macadamia nut flour
1 teaspoon	salt
2 Tablespoons	sugar
2 Tablespoons	egg replacer
1 Tablespoon	xanthan gum
2½ teaspoons	yeast

***Hint:** Grind up approximately ¾ cup macadamia nuts to equal ½ cup of ground flour. If necessary, add 1 Tablespoon of sugar to prevent mixture from becoming a paste.*

Add in:

½ cup	chopped dried pineapple
½ cup	chopped macadamia nuts
¼ cup	shredded or flaked coconut

***FYI:** To enhance the flavor:*

(1) Reconstitute the dried pineapple in pineapple juice for 10 minutes and drain before using.

(2) Toast the macadamia nuts in a 400° oven for 8-10 minutes until they get a little brown.

(3) Toast the coconut for a couple of minutes at 350° until it barely starts to turn brown.

Strawberry and Banana Bread

"Great strawberry shortcake. I topped it with fresh strawberries, vanilla pudding and whipped cream." –Marie

Wet Ingredients: (see page 6)

¾ cup	eggs
¾ cup	water, plus or minus
½ cup	strawberry or banana yogurt
1 teaspoon	cider vinegar
1 teaspoon	vanilla extract
2 Tablespoons	honey

__Hint:__ The fruits make this a very moist bread. Watch your liquid ratio.

Dry Ingredients: (see page 7)

1 cup	white rice flour
½ cup	tapioca starch flour
½ cup	potato starch
¼ cup	soy flour
¼ cup	sweet rice flour
½ cup	millet flour

—or personalize with your favorite flour mix—

1 teaspoon	salt
⅔ cup	dry milk powder
1 Tablespoon	xanthan gum
2 teaspoons	egg replacer
2½ teaspoons	yeast

Add in:

¾ cup	sliced and diced bananas
¾ cup	sliced and diced strawberries

***Recommendation:** This recipe works best when allowed to rise before baking. **Tip:** Keep refrigerated or frozen.*

"Awesome with cream cheese."–Brian

Individual Glaze: See "Beyond Bread," page 138.

Very Berry and Marshmallows Bread

"Layer with blueberries, vanilla ice cream, and whipped cream for a quick dessert." –Vern

Wet Ingredients: (see page 6)

¾ cup	eggs
¾ cup	100% berry fruit juice, plus or minus
½ cup	berry yogurt, any flavor
¼ cup	honey

Dry Ingredients: (see page 7)

1 cup	white rice flour
½ cup	cornstarch
½ cup	tapioca starch flour
½ cup	potato starch
½ cup	sweet rice flour

—or personalize with your favorite flour mix—

1 teaspoon	salt
½ cup	dry milk powder
1 Tablespoon	xanthan gum
2 ½ teaspoons	yeast

Add in:

10 oz.	defrosted, strained mixed berries
1 cup	miniature marshmallows

Hint: *Mix the berries in with the wet ingredients–they are very moist.*

FYI: *If miniature marshmallows are unavailable, cut up the larger marshmallows. To prevent sticking, spray a scissor with a vegetable oil, or rinse the scissor in a glass of warm water between marshmallows.*

Recommendation: *This recipe works best when allowed to rise before baking.* ***Tip:*** *Refrigerate or keep frozen.*

For Baking Methods, see pages 125-132.

White Chocolate and Almonds Bread

"Suggested toppings: Raspberries pureed; orange or raspberry yogurt; chocolate sauce; Grand Marnier or Cointreau"—Chef Charlie Nygaard

Wet Ingredients: (see page 6)

¾ cup	eggs
¾ cup	water, plus or minus
1 teaspoon	plain rice vinegar
½ cup	white chocolate yogurt
2 teaspoons	vanilla extract

Dry Ingredients: (see page 7)

1¼ cups	white rice flour
½ cup	brown rice flour
½ cup	tapioca starch flour
½ cup	potato starch
¼ cup	millet flour

—or personalize with your favorite flour mix—

2 Tablespoons	sweet rice flour
1 teaspoon	salt
2 Tablespoons	dry milk powder
¼ cup	granulated sugar
1 Tablespoon	xanthan gum
2½ teaspoons	yeast

Add in:

½ cup almonds and 8 ounces white chocolate. Use chunks of chocolate for chocolate pockets. Otherwise, use 8 ounces of white chocolate chips.

Hint: *Do not overbake this bread.*

Tip: *Allow to rise before baking, unless you want a cake—then use the No-Knead No-Rise Method*

FYI: *White chocolate is not chocolate at all. It is made from sugar, cocoa butter, milk solids, vanilla and perhaps lecithin. Cheaper versions do not contain any cocoa butter. Consequently their flavor is considered inferior to those that do.*

"This bread was so good, I ate the whole sample piece." —Ron

Zucchini Blueberry Bread

Top with sour cream and blueberries or almond whipped cream.

Wet Ingredients: (see page 6)

¾ cup	eggs
3 Tablespoons	water, plus or minus
1 teaspoon	vinegar
½ cup	yogurt
2 Tablespoons	honey
½ cup	grated and drained zucchini
½ cup	blueberries, drained

***Tip:** Keep bread refrigerated or frozen. This recipe works best when allowed to rise before baking.*

Dry Ingredients: (see page 7)

1 cup	white rice flour
1 cup	tapioca starch flour
½ cup	cornstarch
½ cup	amaranth flour

—or personalize with your favorite flour mix—

1 teaspoon	salt
½ cup	dry milk powder
1 Tablespoon	xanthan gum
2½ teaspoons	yeast

***Hint:** Freeze blueberries and add at the beep to help keep their shape.*

How to Handle Zucchini: Wash the zucchini. Do not remove the skin. Grate as thin as possible. Place on a paper towel and press as much moisture out as possible.

Almond Whipped Cream: See "Beyond Bread," page 135.

Additional Bread Recipe:

Zucchini Chocolate Blueberry Bread

- Add 1 teaspoon chocolate extract
- Add 2 teaspoons Espresso powder
- Add 3 Tablespoons cocoa powder
- Add ½ cup chocolate chips

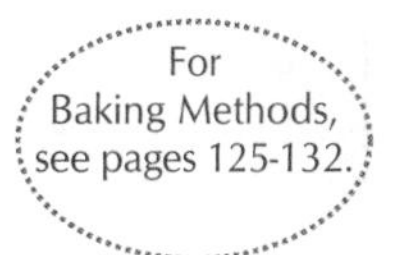
For
Baking Methods,
see pages 125-132.

My Personalized Recipe for: ....

Date:________ Baking method used:________

Amount and type of liquid used:________

Flours or mix used:________

Other changes:________

Notes:________

____

My Personalized Recipe for: ....

Date:________ Baking method used:________

Amount and type of liquid used:________

Flours or mix used:________

Other changes:________

Notes:________

____

My Personalized Recipe for: ....

Date:________ Baking method used:________

Amount and type of liquid used:________

Flours or mix used:________

Other changes:________

Notes:________

____

When personalizing with different flours or ingredients to suit your tastes, diet, for convenience, or for creativity, you may need to adjust the other ingredients.

Bread Machines

All the bread recipes in this book were recipe-tested at least six times, using a minimum of five types of bread machines, in three different parts of the United States, during different times of the year, by at least three, and up to six different recipe Testers.

A total of twelve different bread machine models were used in the testing project.

The recipes in this book worked for us in every bread machine we used. Once you know how to control the liquid ratio of your bread, you can feel confident the recipes will work for you, too

Here are a couple of the things you need to know about bread machines.

1. You do not need to pay top dollar for a bread machine
2. We used three garage sale machines. Two of them worked beautifully, and they didn't even come with a manual! The third machine we threw away. It took almost 4.5 hours to make the bread and the texture left much to be desired.
3. My favorite machine was purchased for less than $50.00. Most machines were only slightly above that range. Each machine had features that were helpful, as well as shortfalls.
4. Both of the $200.00 range machines made delicious bread. I was happier with one machine's performance more than the other due to its wider programmability; its horizontal loaf shape yielded more slices of bread; and the dual paddles appeared to mix the dough better. Yet those dual paddles were the cause of overmixing a bread or two, (i.e. the Cream of Rice™ Bread) resulting in a crumbly loaf.

5. Every bread machine operates a little differently, even though they all have the same basic elements.

   Basic elements: Think of the bread machine as a mini-oven, with a heating element, a bread pan and some buttons that control how long the breads mix, knead, rise and bake.

   The major differences in the machines are the different options for how to bake the bread. Some machines simply have a basic-cycle control panel and options are limited (but still work for us) while others let you program every step of the way.

   The minor differences include the amount of yeast needed to make the bread rise varied by a ½ teaspoon, and the amount of water varied by a tablespoon or two in different machines. One of the seven machines I used needed an extra

10 minutes to completely bake the bread. These differences are referred to as minor, since you will probably be using only one bread machine and will quickly become familiar with the amount of yeast, liquid and time it will take to produce the best loaf of bread possible.

6. Look for a bread machine that will fit your needs and pocketbook.
   - Think of size and shape—how it will fit under your cabinets and on your counter. Then consider the length of cord you will need to reach an outlet.
   - Look for a machine that has a Basic Cycle, a separate Dough Cycle, and a separate Bake Cycle, if you want to try all the baking methods in this book. If you only have a Basic Cycle on your present machine—use it and decide for yourself how you like the results before you invest in a different machine.
   - Breads in this book take between 60 to 75 minutes to bake. Make certain you have that long a bake cycle or the machine will allow you to add baking minutes if the bread is not done.
   - Consider a bread machine with the largest window possible for easy viewing.

The recipes in this book, except for the Basic Sandwich Bread Recipe, were based on a medium-sized loaf, approximately 1½ pound, so they will work in most bread machines.

I. One Step Method—Bread Machine

Using the Basic Cycle

Time: approximately 3½ hours

This is Denise's favorite method–see her story and technique on page 155.

1. Mix wet ingredients together in a bowl and set aside.
2. Mix dry ingredients together in a separate bowl, except for the yeast.
3. Or use Denise's technique and measure everything directly into the bread pan instead of into separate preliminary bowls.
4. Put ingredients into the bread machine pan in the order given by the manufacturer. Depending on your machine instructions, usually the yeast is put in last, on top of the dry ingredients.
5. Select Basic Cycle, and then press the Start button.
6. During the first 7–10 minutes help the paddle mix the dough once or twice by using a rubber spatula to scrape the dough off the sides of the pan and out of the corners.
7. As the paddle mixes, intermittently check to make certain the dough is spreading to the sides of the pan. If the dough is not spreading out, add a tablespoon of water at a time. Allow the dough to absorb the water before adding more. You can help mix by using a spatula, if you so choose.
8. After 10–12 minutes, you should be able to see thin paddle lines on the top of the dough as the paddle spins around. The dough should have spread to the sides of the pan, due to the liquid adjustment in step 7. You may also see a small "cap" on top of the paddle, depending on how your machine operates. The dough will develop a somewhat silky, shiny look.
9. If you add raisins, chocolate chips, vegetables, nuts, or so on, in the beginning of the mixing process, you will need to develop an eye for looking beyond those ingredients to determine if your dough is the right consistency. Some recipe Testers add everything in the beginning, some wait 10 minutes, or for the beep.
10. The dough should not be in a ball. It should not look dry. If it does, add warm water one tablespoon at a time. Allow enough time for the dough to absorb the water before adding more.
11. Depending on your machine, or the Basic Cycle programming, it will mix and knead the ingredients. Then the machine program will allow the dough to rise, and then the paddle(s) will punch the dough down, and let it rise again. Then the machine will bake the dough.

12. When the Basic Cycle is done, and before you turn the machine off, check to make certain the bread is baked through. Insert a toothpick into the center–if it comes out clean, it is an indication the bread is done. Or if you tap on the crust, it should sound hollow. Ordinarily, the crust should not be soft. If in doubt, bake an additional 10 minutes and retest.
13. After the bread has baked, remove the bread pan from the bread machine. Allow to cool on a wire rack for 10 minutes, then turn the bread pan upside down and shake out the bread.
14. The paddle may or may not stick inside the bread. Do not worry, it can be easily removed either while your bread is warm, or after it has cooled.

Note: Steps and terminology for different machines or models may vary, along with programmed cycle times.

II. Two Step Method—Bread Machine

Using Dough-Bake Cycles

Time: approximately 2½ hours

This is Charlene's favorite method–see her story and technique on page 156.

1. Mix all wet ingredients together in a bowl and set aside.
2. Mix dry ingredients together in a separate bowl, except for the yeast.
3. Or use Denise's technique and measure everything directly into the bread pan instead of into separate preliminary bowls.
4. Put the ingredients into the bread machine pan in the order given by the manufacturer. Depending on your machine instructions, usually the yeast is put in last, on top of the dry ingredients.
5. Select Dough, and then press Start.
6. During the first 7–10 minutes, help the paddle mix the dough once or twice by using a rubber spatula to scrape the dough off the sides of the pan and out of the corners.
7. As the paddle mixes, intermittently check to make certain the dough is spreading to the sides of the pan. If the dough is not spreading out, add a tablespoon of water at a time. Allow the dough to absorb the water before adding more. You can help mix by using a spatula, if you so choose.
8. After 10–12 minutes, you should be able to see thin paddle lines on the top of the dough as the paddle spins around. The dough should have spread to the sides of the pan, due to the liquid adjustment in step 7. You may also see a small "cap" on top of the paddle, depending on how your machine operates. The dough will develop a somewhat silky, shiny look.

9. If you add raisins, chocolate chips, vegetables, nuts, or so on in the beginning of the mixing process, you will need to develop an eye for looking beyond those ingredients to determine if your dough is the right consistency. Some recipe Testers add everything in the beginning, some wait 10 minutes or for the beep.
10. The dough should not be in a ball. It should not look dry. If it does, add warm water one tablespoon at a time. Allow enough time for the dough to absorb the water before adding more.
11. The machine Dough Cycle will ordinarily mix, and then knead the dough for approximately 20–40 minutes. The machine programming will then allow the dough to rise for 50–60 minutes.
12. When the Dough Cycle is complete, press Stop.
13. Select Bake and then press the Start button. If you can set the length of time your machine will bake, set it for 70–75 minutes. Begin checking if the bread is done after 60 minutes.
14. Some machines will allow you to program a light, medium or dark crust.
15. When the Bake cycle is done, check to make certain the bread is baked through. Insert a toothpick into the center–if it comes out clean, it is an indication the bread is done. Or if you tap on the crust, it should sound hollow. Ordinarily, the crust should not be soft. If in doubt, bake for an additional 10 minutes and retest.
16. After the bread has baked, remove the bread pan from the bread machine. Allow to cool on a wire rack for 10 minutes, then turn the bread pan upside down and shake out the bread.
17. The paddle may or may not stick inside the bread. Don't worry, it can be easily removed either while your bread is warm, or after it has cooled.

Note: Steps and terminology for different machines or models may vary, along with programmed cycle times.

III. No-Knead No-Rise Method—Bread Machine

Using a Short Mix Cycle and Full Bake Cycle

Time: approximately 1½ hours

This is one of Bruce's favorite methods—see his story and technique on page 158.

1. Mix all wet ingredients together in a bowl and set aside
2. Mix all dry ingredients together in a separate bowl, except for the yeast.
3. Add 1 teaspoon baking soda and 1 Tablespoon baking powder to the dry ingredients. Add the yeast to the dry ingredients.
4. Put ingredients into the bread machine pan in the order given by the manufacturer—or, you may measure all the ingredients directly into the pan in the order suggested by the manufacturer.
5. Select any of the machine programs that will mix the ingredients together. For instance, select Basic Cycle or the Dough cycle. Then press the Start button.
6. Allow the bread machine to mix the dough together, approximately 7–10 minutes. Do not allow the machine to mix or knead the dough for 20–30 minutes. That is too long a time for this method. **The baking powder/baking soda/yeast combination must start baking quickly.** Too long a mix time will lessen the rise of the bread.
7. Help the paddle mix the dough by using a rubber spatula during the 5–7 minutes of mix time. Since this is a short mix time, do not omit this step.
8. As the paddle mixes, make certain the ingredients are forming a mixture that spreads to the sides of the pan. After 7–10 minutes, you should be able to see the dough as thoroughly mixed. It is possible you may not see the thin paddle lines on top of the dough as in other methods, due to the short mixing time.
9. If you added raisins, chocolate chips, vegetables, nuts or so on, immediately into your dry or wet ingredients, you will need to develop an eye for looking beyond those ingredients to determine if your dough is the right consistency. Some recipe Testers add everything in the beginning, some wait 5 minutes.
10. The dough should not be in a ball. It should not look dry. If it does, add water one tablespoon at a time. Allow the dough to absorb the water before adding more.
11. Stop the cycle once the ingredients are thoroughly mixed together, the dough is spreading to the sides of the pan, and there are no lumps, approximately 7–10 minutes. Recognize some machines may need a longer mix time due to the size of the paddle or strength of the motor.

It is best to help the machine mix and make any liquid adjustments within the first 5–7 minutes.

12. After the dough has mixed, do not allow rise time. Select Bake and then press the Start button. If you can set the length of time your machine will bake, set it for 70 minutes and begin checking the bread for doneness after 60 minutes.

13. Some machines will allow you to program a light, medium or dark crust.

14. When the Bake cycle is complete, check to make certain the bread is baked through. Insert a toothpick into the center–if it comes out clean, it is an indication the bread is done. Or if you tap on the crust, it should sound hollow. Ordinarily, the crust should not be soft. If in doubt, bake an additional 10 minutes and retest.

15. After the bread has baked, remove the bread pan from the bread machine. Allow to cool on a wire rack for 10 minutes, then turn the bread pan upside down and shake out the bread.

16. The paddle may or may not stick inside the bread. Don't worry, it can be easily removed either while your bread is warm, or after it has cooled.

Note: Steps and terminology for different machines or models may vary, along with programmed cycle times.

Oven Baking Methods

All the recipes in this book may be baked in the oven. You can create:

- A full loaf of bread in a bread pan
- A round loaf of bread in a cake pan
- Personal-sized breads in small bread pans
- Large rolls using muffin rings
- Dinner-sized rolls using a muffin pan
- Appetizer-sized rolls in mini-muffin pans
- Hamburger and hot dog buns in forms
- Pizza using a round pizza pan
- Foccacia in a jelly roll pan

The following is some basic information for baking in a standard kitchen oven.

1. Check your oven temperature. Place a thermometer in the center of your oven. Turn your oven dial to 350° and allow the oven to warm for 30 minutes. Check the thermometer. Does the thermometer register 350°? If not, adjust your oven dial until the inside registers 350°. Now you know how many degree difference there is between the inside of your oven and the dial setting. (All temps are in Fahrenheit.)

   The Testers baked the breads in this book in 350° ovens.

2. Determine which bread method you plan to use:

   - **Rise Method using Yeast:** Mix the dough ingredients together, allow the dough to rise until it has almost doubled in size. This could take 15 minutes to 1 hour. Then bake.
   - **No-Knead No-Rise Method:** In addition to the yeast, add 1 teaspoon baking soda and 1 Tablespoon baking powder to the dry ingredients in the recipe. Mix the dough ingredients together, and then bake. Omit the rise time.

3. Decide how you want to mix the dough:

   If you are using a counter mixer to mix the dough, use the large bowl and regular beaters. A dough hook is not necessary. Put the wet ingredients in first, blend together on low, and then slowly add the dry ingredients. Turn the mixer to medium speed and beat for 3–5 minutes, until it is very smooth. The dough will look pasty, or like a thick cake batter.

If your dough is too thick, add a tablespoon of warm water at a time. Allow enough time for the mixer to incorporate the liquid before adding any more water.

What about the yeast? The yeast can be handled a couple of different ways.

- My preferred method is to add the yeast directly to the dry ingredients. Look at your yeast package to see if it provides that option.
- Another method is to proof the yeast. Set aside approximately ½ cup of water from your recipe and warm it to 105–110°. Add ½ teaspoon of sugar. When the sugar is dissolved, add 2¼ teaspoons of yeast and stir until the yeast is wet. Within 5–8 minutes, the yeast should be foamy. Add the foamy yeast to the wet ingredients.
- If you are using the No-Knead No-Rise Method, the yeast will be added last, along with the 1 teaspoon baking soda and 1 tablespoon baking powder, to the dry ingredients. Add the dry ingredients to the wet ingredients.

A Special Note on the No-Knead No-Rise Method: Once the baking powder, baking soda and yeast have been added to the wet ingredients, the dough will need to be mixed and placed in the oven within a relatively sort period of time, or the effectiveness will dissipate, resulting in a lower rise.

If you are using a bread machine to mix the dough, put the ingredients into the pan in the order recommended by the manufacturer. See the "Bread Machine" section for more information.

Question: *Why would someone use a bread machine for mixing or allowing the dough to rise when they plan to bake it in the oven?*

People use the bread machine for many reasons. For instance, perhaps they do not own a counter mixer; they cannot lift the counter mixer bowls; the bread machine is handy; they believe they get a better consistency from the machine; or the bread rises better; or they would rather clean the bread machine pan than a mixing bowl and beaters.

You may also allow the dough to rise in the bread machine. See the "Bread Machine" section for more information.

4. Prep your pans for the oven by lightly coating the inside with a vegetable oil, solid shortening, butter or a cooking oil spray. Some of the Testers chose to dust the pans with rice flour, some did not.

5. If the dough is rising outside of the bread machine, remember to put it in a warm place that is free from drafts. Allow the dough to rise to almost twice its size. This can take from 15 minutes or 1 hour, depending on the yeast used and the temperature in your kitchen. The dough will finish rising while it is in the oven.

   The No-Knead No-Rise Method, with the yeast, baking soda and baking powder, omits the rising time.

6. Bake in the oven at 350° for 60–75 minutes for a full loaf of bread and 30–45 minutes for the smaller loaves and rolls.

   After a loaf of bread has baked for 35–45 minutes, cover it with aluminum foil so the crust does not get too brown.

7. Check to make certain the bread is done. Insert a toothpick into the center and hold it for two seconds. If it is free of any stickiness when it comes out, that is an indication the bread is done. Or, if you tap on the crust, it should sound hollow. Ordinarily, the crust should not be soft. If in doubt, bake an additional 10 minutes and test again.

8. When the bread is done, remove it from the oven. Allow to cool on a wire rack for 4–7 minutes, then turn pan upside down and shake out the bread.

Beyond Bread

This chapter contains a variety of bread icings, glazes, sauces, butters, spreads, sandwich suggestions and side dishes or entrees to accompany the breads in this book. Some of the bread recipes suggest toppings to further develop the bread's theme or as an interesting contrast. You will find these recipes to be suitable for many breads or occasions. Some of the recipes are loosely constructed so you may tailor them to your particular usage and tastes.

We would enjoy hearing what original toppings you have used on the breads in this book. Suggestions may be placed on this book's companion website for all to enjoy.

Almond Whipped Cream:
In a chilled mixing bowl, beat 2 cups chilled heavy whipping cream with ½ cup powdered sugar, and 2 teaspoons pure almond extract until stiff. Or choose vanilla extract or rum as the flavoring.

Artichoke Spread:
Finely chop a can of drained artichoke hearts. Mix together with 2 teaspoons of minced garlic, 1 Tablespoon basil, 1 teaspoon oregano, 1 Tablespoon chopped tomato and 1-2 Tablespoons extra virgin olive oil. Spread on bread.

Bacon and Egg Salad Entrée:
Combine 4 chopped, hard-cooked eggs in a bowl with ½ cup mayonnaise, 2 Tablespoons of sweet pickle relish and 1 teaspoon prepared mustard. Blend well. Place four pieces of lightly toasted Bacon and Eggs Bread on a cookie sheet. Lay an optional slice or two of bacon on top of the bread. Top with ¼ cup of the egg mixture. Sprinkle with 2 Tablespoons of shredded Sharp Cheddar cheese. Bake at 350° for about 5-7 minutes or until cheese is melted. Serve with a cup of fruit.

Blue Cornmeal Chicken Beignets:
Soak 1 pound of very thin chicken breast strips in milk for 2-3 hours in the refrigerator. Remove chicken from the milk and blot dry.

Lightly whisk two eggs together and place in a shallow bowl. Put 1 cup rice flour in a shallow bowl and 1 cup blue cornmeal in a third shallow bowl.

Dip each chicken breast strip in rice flour seasoned with salt and pepper and shake off any excess. Then dip the chicken strip in the beaten eggs. Lastly, dip strip into blue cornmeal and carefully fry in 4 Tablespoons of hot oil for 12 minutes, turning once, or bake in a 350° oven until done. (Frying gives the best results) Serve atop Santa Fe Blue Cornmeal Bread spread with honey. Add a dollop of Dressed Up Mayonnaise.

Bruschetta Spread:
Combine together 8 diced plum tomatoes, ½ cup chopped fresh basil, ½ cup minced red onion, salt and pepper to taste. Rub warm crostini with garlic clove, then top with mixture.

Caribbean Picadillo (Ground Beef) Entrée:
In 1 Tablespoon of olive oil, add 1 cup finely chopped onion and 1 cup minced red, yellow or green bell pepper. Cook until onion is translucent, about 5 minutes. Add 2 Tablespoons minced garlic (or to taste) and cook for 1 minute. Add 1 pound extra lean ground beef and cook until browned, stirring frequently. Add ½ cup water, 1 teaspoon hot sauce, 1/3 cup raisins, ¼ cup pimiento stuffed olives, ½ cup tomato paste, ½ teaspoon ground cumin, ½ teaspoon ground cinnamon, salt and pepper to taste. Simmer, stirring frequently, until desired consistency. Serve with white rice, black beans and Caribbean Sweet Bread, or bread of your choice.

Cheddar Cheese and Onion Sandwich

1 sweet onion thinly sliced
2 cups grated cheddar cheese
1 cup grated zucchini
½ teaspoon dried basil
½ teaspoon dry mustard
1 cup bacon, cooked to crispy and crumbled

Heat oven to 350°. Mix all the above ingredients together except for the onion. On ungreased cookie sheet place Cheddar and Onion bread slices. Put 1 slice of onion on top each piece. Spoon mixture on top of onion. Bake for 5 minutes or until cheese has melted. Makes 4- 6 servings.

Chocolate Hazelnut Spread:

Toast 1/3 cup hazelnuts and process them in a food processor until they become a meal. Set aside. Combine ½ cup of sweetened condensed milk, ½ cup semisweet chocolate chips and 3 Tablespoons of honey or light corn syrup in the top of a double boiler. Heat until the chocolate chips have melted, about 3 minutes. Add the hot chocolate mixture to the hazelnut meal and process in the food processor until it is smooth. Spread over the Chocolate Cherry Bread for a great dessert.

Chopped Ham Spread:

1 package (3oz) cream cheese, 2 Tablespoons finely chopped ham; 1 Tablespoon shredded Swiss cheese and ½ teaspoon prepared mustard.

Cinnamon Butter:

Combine one stick of softened butter (8 tablespoons), 1 teaspoon maple syrup, a drop or two of vanilla, a sprinkle or two of cinnamon and a dash of sugar. Combine all together and refrigerate until ready to use.

Cinnamon Icing:

Combine ½ cup powdered sugar, ¼ teaspoon cinnamon, 2 teaspoons water. Drizzle over hot crust.

Crab and Dill Spread:

1 cup crab meat
¼ cup pine nuts
½ cup minced bell pepper
1 Tablespoon finely minced green onion
1 Tablespoon finely minced celery
1 teaspoon lemon juice
1 teaspoon dill weed
¼ cup finely shredded Swiss or Gruyere cheese
½ cup plain yogurt, sour cream or mayonnaise

Blend all together and spread on Dill and Cottage Cheese Bread, or bread of your choice.

Cranberry Spread:

Combine together:

¼ cup chopped celery
1 small shallot, finely chopped
½ cup chopped toasted pecans
1 Tablespoon finely chopped tarragon leaves
½ cup sour cream
salt and pepper

Spread over bread. Layer a slice of chicken breast, eggplant or cucumbers atop the spread. Sprinkle with salt and pepper. Top with lettuce.

Curried Apricot Spread:

Puree 1 can of drained apricot halves. In a small saucepan, combine the puree with 1 cup of apricot yogurt and ½ teaspoon of curry powder. Add 1 teaspoon of cornstarch to the mixture. Bring to a boil, and stir constantly until thickened. Chill.

Curried Chicken Salad Spread:

Mix together 1 cup diced pre-cooked chicken breast, 2 Tablespoons raisins (grapes cut in half would also be good), ½ to 1 teaspoon sweet curry powder, 2 teaspoons mango chutney, approximately ½ cup mayonnaise to make salad as moist as you desire, and 1 Tablespoon chopped cashew nuts. Chill.

Dressed Up Mayonnaise:
Dress up mayonnaise by adding 1 teaspoon of your favorite mustard to ¼ cup mayonnaise. Or blend together 1 teaspoon of horseradish with 1 Tablespoon of mustard.

Easy Mexican Rice:
Saute 1 cup long grain rice in 1 Tablespoon oil until it becomes golden in color. Add 1 Tablespoon chopped garlic and ½ cup finely chopped onion. Brown for 1 minute. Add a can of diced tomatoes or salsa, 2½ cups water or gluten-free chicken broth, 1 cup finely diced carrots and a pinch of salt. Cover and simmer until rice is cooked.

Egg-in-Hole Breakfast Entrée:
Cut a hole in the center of one of the pieces of bread—not too big, about 1″ or so. Then butter one side of the bread and lay it onto the warm griddle. Fry lightly until it starts to toast. Spread butter on the second side with a brush. Turn the bread over and lightly fry. Break one egg into a bowl and slide it into the hole of the bread. Cover the pan and cook until it meets your fried-egg criteria. If you like, turn the bread over to fry on the other side. Top with a slice of cheese or ham.

Garden Sandwich:
Combine cottage cheese with diced green chilies and sunflower seeds. Spread on the bread. Top with alfalfa sprouts, sunflower seeds and tomatoes.

Garlic Aioli:
Mix together 1 cup mayonnaise, ¼ cup lemon juice, 4 minced garlic cloves and 1 Tablespoon Dijon mustard. Put in food processor and pulse until well mixed. Makes about 1½ cups.

Ginger Spread:
In a small bowl, mash together 3 Tablespoons of unsalted butter and 2 teaspoons of finely minced ginger. Combine thoroughly. Spread on lightly warmed bread.

Green Onion Scramble Entrée:
Scramble two eggs with green onion, a dusting of curry powder and some melted cheddar cheese. Layer atop toasted Seed Bread and crown with a grilled tomato slice.

Grilled Bird and Beef Sandwich:
Layer the bread with mayonnaise sprinkled with flaxseed. Add smoked turkey, horseradish, roast beef, cheddar cheese, havarti cheese, butter lettuce, beefsteak tomato, salt and freshly ground pepper.

Grilled Eggplant Sandwich:
Smooth Garlic Aioli on a lightly toasted piece of Buckwheat Pumpernickel Bread. Add grilled eggplant, roasted red peppers, and caramelized red onion. Top with mozzarella cheese and tuck under the broiler until the cheese melts.

Grilled Pineapple, Tuna and Cheese Sandwich:
Place one piece of rye bread on a paper plate (to absorb the moisture from the bread). Lightly brush top side of the bread with mayonnaise, olive oil or butter. Arrange a drained pineapple slice on top of the rye bread; add ¼ cup drained tuna fish over the pineapple. Top with a slice of cheddar cheese. Microwave until the cheese starts to melt.

Grilled Tomato, Avocado and Muenster Sandwich:
Combine in a bowl:
- 1 Tablespoon finely minced red onion
- 3 Tablespoons sour cream
- 1 Tablespoon Dijon mustard

Butter one side each of two slices of Mashed Potato and Cheese Bread. Spread the mustard mixture over the unbuttered side of the bread. Top the mustard mixture side with two tomato slices, mashed avocado and 1 piece of Muenster Cheese. Lay the second bread slice on top of the cheese with the buttered side up. Grill in a large skillet for 2 minutes or until golden brown, gently flip and grill the other side until golden brown.

Hannah's Healthy Sandwich:
Layer light mayonnaise, cucumbers, tomatoes, butter lettuce, pineapple slices, and ham on a piece of bread. Or layer smooth goat cheese with roasted bell peppers and turkey over toasted bread.

Herb Cheese Butter:
Combine together:
- ¼ cup softened butter
- 1 Tablespoon grated Parmesan Cheese
- 1 teaspoon chopped fresh parsley
- ¼ teaspoon dried oregano leaves
- dash of garlic salt

Honey Grilled Cheese:
Slice a piece of Swiss cheese and set aside. Spread honey on one piece of bread. On a second piece of bread spread peanut butter. Put the bread together with the spread sides facing each other and the Swiss Cheese in between. Lightly butter bottom side of bread and grill until golden brown. Butter the top side of the bread and flip the sandwich over to brown the second side.

Honey Walnut Spread:
Combine 3 oz. (6 Tablespoons) of cream cheese, 2 teaspoons of honey and 1 Tablespoon chopped walnuts or pecans. Mix all together and smooth on top of the Brown Rice Bread.

Hummus Spread:
There are many variations of the hummus spread. Make your own version by mashing a can of chickpeas (or black beans). Season to taste with lemon juice, olive oil, and garlic. Cumin and coriander may be added, or chipolte puree for a spicier version. Or add tahini (sesame seeds ground into a paste) and pine nuts. Serve warmed or at room temperature as a spread or bread dip.

Individual Glaze:
Make an individual-sized glaze mixture by combining ¼ cup confectioner sugar, 1 teaspoon of melted better, a dash of almond extract and enough milk to allow it to drizzle over the bread.

Lemon Icing:
Combine together:
- 1 cup confectioners sugar
- 1 teaspoon lemon juice
- 2 Tablespoons sugar
- 1 teaspoon lemon liqueur (triple sec)
- 1 teaspoon lemon extract

Beat with an electric mixer until thick and creamy. Adjust consistency as needed with lemon juice. Brush on bread.

Lemon Orange Glaze:
- ½ cup sugar
- 1 Tablespoon cornstarch
- 2 teaspoons rice flour
- ½ cup orange juice
- ¼ cup apple juice
- 2 teaspoons butter
- 2 teaspoons orange peel
- 2 teaspoons lemon peel

Mix the sugar with the cornstarch in a small pan. As it turns to liquid, slowly add the juices, and the remainder of the ingredients. Bring to a boil, stirring constantly. Once it reaches boiling, remove from heat and very lightly drizzle over bread. This works best on breads that will be enjoyed within a short period of time.

Mandarin Orange Spread:
Mix together crumbled goat cheese, mandarin oranges, pine nuts and a touch of apricot orange marmalade. Add diced chicken or turkey if you like. Add a bit of mayonnaise if you want a creamy spread. Spread on Citrus Zest Bread and top with butter lettuce. Mmmm good!

Mushroom and Asparagus Duxelle:

¼ cup butter
2 Tablespoons minced shallots
2 cloves garlic, minced
1 pound fresh mushrooms, finely chopped or ground
2 Tablespoons parsley
1 teaspoon chives
1 teaspoon rosemary
1 teaspoon basil
salt and pepper
¾ cup heavy cream

Melt butter and sauté onions and garlic for 3-4 minutes. Add mushrooms and sauté, stirring frequently. Allow to simmer until moisture has evaporated. Add herbs and seasoning and continue to simmer for a couple of minutes. Add cream and incorporate well. Allow mixture to reduce to desired consistency to pour over toasted Rice and White Rice Bread, or use as a sauce for vegetables or on a baked potato.

Heartier Duxelle: Thinly slice and sauté a mixture of red, yellow and green peppers. Brown ½ pound of sausage and add the sautéed peppers. Add to the Duxelle. You may need additional heavy cream.

Onion Muffuletta Sandwich:
Prepare the olive mixture by chopping the following extra fine.

1 cup chopped sweet onion
½ cup pimento stuffed green olives
¼ cup extra virgin olive oil
1 clove crushed garlic
1 Tablespoon red wine vinegar
1 Tablespoon drained capers
1 teaspoon each oregano and parsley
1 Tablespoon dried basil

Spread the muffuletta olive mixture over bread and layer Provolone cheese, Genoa salami, ham and mortadella on top.

Orange-Cranberry Sauce:
In a skillet, mix together 2 Tablespoons of brown sugar, 1/3 cup of orange juice and 1 cup fresh or frozen cranberries. Cook until the cranberries pop, or about 5 minutes. Stir in ¼ cup raisins and 2 Tablespoons of orange-flavored liqueur (Cointreau) or 1 Tablespoon orange juice and 1 Tablespoon lemon juice. Add ¼ cup lightly toasted pine nuts. Ladle over warmed bread. Serve immediately.

Peanut Butter Glaze:
Combine ½ cup confectioner sugar with ¼ cup peanut butter and 2 Tablespoons milk. Spread over the top of Peanut Butter and Banana Bread or the bread of your choice–either as a crust topping or as a spread.

Pimento Cheese Spread:

1 cup finely grated cheddar cheese
6 ounces (¾ cup) softened cream cheese
¼ cup chopped green olives
¼ cup diced pimentos
1 teaspoon sugar
salt and pepper to taste
onion salt to taste
garlic salt to taste

Combine together the cheddar cheese, cream cheese, olives and pimentos. Add seasonings. Beat with a mixer until fluffy. Add milk or mayonnaise if desired. Refrigerate.

Pizza Appetizer/Entrée:
Lightly toast the Pizza Slice Bread. Cut in half or quarters. Top with goat cheese, sun-dried tomatoes, fresh basil and smoked salmon. Serve at room temperature.

Pork Chops and Sauerkraut Entrée:
Layer peeled and quartered potatoes at the bottom of a roaster pan. Add sliced carrots and diced rutabagas. Add pork chops that have been seared and browned in a fry pan. Cover with sauerkraut, sauerkraut liquid and 1 cup of water. Cover and roast at 350° until the potatoes and carrots are done, approximately 1½ hours.

Pumpkin Butter:

Beat ½ cup softened butter with ¼ cup sifted powdered sugar, ½ cup canned pumpkin, ¼ teaspoon ground cinnamon and ¼ teaspoon ground nutmeg, until fluffy. Spread on Pumpkin Bread.

Quick Potato Salad:

Use canned small whole or sliced potatoes. They are easy, delicious, and available on most supermarket shelves. Combine them with all your other favorite potato salad ingredients.

Reuben in a Dish:

1 pound sauerkraut, drained
1 teaspoon caraway seeds
¾ pound corned beef, thinly sliced
1 cup finely shredded Swiss cheese
½ cup mayonnaise
¼ cup Thousand Island dressing
2 slices gluten-free pumpernickel bread, cubed
2 Tablespoons melted butter
2 tomatoes, seeded and chopped

In 2 quart casserole, combine sauerkraut and caraway seeds; spread evenly in bottom. Layer with corned beef and cheese. Combine mayonnaise and Thousand Island dressing and spread over the cheese. Toss bread cubes with butter; sprinkle bread cubes and tomatoes over top. Bake in preheated 350° oven until heated through (45–55 min).

Ricotta Cheese Spread:

Combine together:

5 ounces (2/3 cup) Ricotta Cheese
2 Tablespoons orange juice
½ teaspoon cinnamon
1/3 cup raisins, cranberries, cherries or raspberries
2 Tablespoons nuts
1 teaspoon honey
1-2 drops vanilla extract

Stuffed Mushrooms for Sandwich or Appetizer:

Combine together in a small mixing bowl

1 can of drained white crabmeat
½ cup shredded Parmesan cheese
2 teaspoons parsley
dash of salt and pepper
pinch of garlic powder
onion powder to taste
1 teaspoon of fresh lemon juice
½ cup of gluten-free bread crumbs.

Pour ¾ stick (6 Tablespoons) of melted butter over the mixture, and mix just until moist. If too moist, add more cheese or bread crumbs. If not moist enough, add more melted butter.

Remove stem from bite-sized mushrooms. Chop stems and add to the stuffing mixture. Brush olive oil on the inside of the mushroom cap. Fill the mushroom cap with the mixture.

Top with a small slice of Swiss cheese, and then add more stuffing mixture over the cheese. Sprinkle with paprika and put under the broiler until warmed; the crumbs turn a golden brown and are heated through. The mushrooms will be limp.

Swedish Meatball Sandwich:

Combine together ½ cup of gluten-free bread crumbs or crackers, ½ cup cream, 2 Tablespoons of melted unsalted butter, 1 Tablespoon minced onion, 1/3 lb. each of ground beef, veal and pork, 1 egg, a dash of nutmeg, a pinch of salt and pepper. Form into meatballs and sauté until browned on the outside, then bake at 350° until done. Slice in half or serve whole on Limpa Rye bread.

Thousand Island Salad Dressing—Homemade:

Combine 1 cup mayonnaise, 1 Tablespoon ketchup, ½ teaspoon paprika, ½ teaspoon vinegar, 1 Tablespoon chopped red pepper or 1 Tablespoon sweet relish, and ½ Tablespoon chives. Use as dressing or as a spread.

Tofu Spread

1 package firm extra silky tofu, crumbled
½ cup mayonnaise
2 Tablespoons diced chives
1 small carrot, diced very fine
1 diced red bell pepper
1 chopped celery stalk
¼ cup unsalted sunflower seeds
1 teaspoon curry powder
1 teaspoon turmeric
1 teaspoon garlic powder
1 Tablespoon gluten-free soy sauce

Combine all together. Serve on bread with sprouts.

Traditional Open-Faced Turkey Sandwich:

Simply layer any variation of mayonnaise, cranberries, stuffing and thinly sliced turkey. Season with salt and pepper. Cover with warm gravy made with arrowroot or cornstarch. Serve with mashed potatoes and green beans.

Tuna Nicoise Sandwich:

Drain one can of tuna packed in olive oil. Combine with 2 Tablespoons of drained and sliced black olives. 2 teaspoons finely chopped onions, 2 Tablespoons of mayonnaise, 1 hard boiled egg finely chopped, garlic salt, pepper, and ½ cup shredded mozzarella cheese. Add a Tablespoon of drained capers, if desired. Mix well. Spread on Sour Cream and Chives Bread. Add a tomato sprinkled lightly with pepper. Top with butter lettuce and present with French Green Beans. Who can resist?

Veggie Sandwich:

Layer mayonnaise, Chevre goat cheese, baby spinach leaves, sliced heirloom tomatoes, and thinly sliced unpeeled cucumber on Brown Rice Bread. Season with salt and pepper if desired.

Recipes generously contributed by Jeanne Basye, Chef Charlie Nygaard, Bernice Pepin, Geraldine Lang, Chef Tanya Chakravarty, Linda Taroli, and others.

My Personalized Recipe for: . . . .

Date:________________ Baking method used:________________________

Amount and type of liquid used:________________________________

Flours or mix used:____

Other changes:____

Notes:____

____

My Personalized Recipe for: . . . .

Date:________________ Baking method used:________________________

Amount and type of liquid used:________________________________

Flours or mix used:____

Other changes:____

Notes:____

____

My Personalized Recipe for: . . . .

Date:________________ Baking method used:________________________

Amount and type of liquid used:________________________________

Flours or mix used:____

Other changes:____

Notes:____

____

When personalizing with different flours or ingredients to suit your tastes, diet, for convenience, or for creativity, you may need to adjust the other ingredients.

Frequently Asked Questions

Question: The Meal-in-a-Slice Breads are so interesting. Where did the idea come from?

Answer: Meal-in-a-Slice Breads is our answer to gluten "stuffed" breads that are popular in Italian, Greek, Baltic Nation cuisines, as well as others. They make great picnic and travel food as they can be baked and double wrapped in foil to keep warm. They also keep well in the refrigerator. If you get hungry, just slice, heat and serve. They make for a satisfying meal or snack.

Question: How is freshly baked gluten-free bread stored?

Answer: Gluten-free breads have a shorter counter and freezer life than gluten breads, particularly because they have no preservatives. Almost everyone has their own special technique to make the bread last as long as possible. Here are just a few of the techniques:

- Keep the bread on the counter for as long as you can. Perhaps two to three days. Then refrigerate it for two more days. If any is left, wrap it in a double freezer bag and freeze it.
- As soon as the bread has cooled, cut the loaf into individual slices and wrap each slice in aluminum foil. Place them in a freezer bag and tuck it inside the freezer.
- Separate the cut loaf into two pieces. Keep one-half in the refrigerator. Wrap the second half in a cling wrap, then in aluminum foil and freeze.

When I bake a loaf of bread, I plan on taking sandwiches to work that week, so I rarely need to freeze it.

Question: How is the bread defrosted?

Answer: Since there are so many different toaster ovens, toasters, and microwaves, you will need to determine what works for you. The following are quotes and some of the techniques that people use:

- Take your bread immediately from the freezer and put it in your non-preheated convection oven, directly on the rack. Turn the temperature to 350° and allow baking until it is soft and warmed, about 3 minutes.
- My toaster oven has a defrost cycle. I turn it to "Defrost" and then "Toast." It takes 7 minutes for a perfectly defrosted toasted piece of bread. Some breads make better toast than others.

- Place the frozen bread on a paper plate. Allow it to thaw on the counter for about 15 minutes. This works for me unless I forget it is there. Then it gets hard.
- My microwave has a defrost cycle. If I put the frozen piece of bread on a paper plate, it will defrost at half power within 2 minutes, and will not be dry.
- Sometimes just sprinkling a little bit of water on the frozen bread before you pop it in the oven or toaster seems to help it retain its moisture while it is defrosting.

Question: What information does the companion website, www.lynnrae.com have?

Answer: The companion website is a way for you to share your suggested bread uses, toppings, storage or defrosting techniques with others. You can also share any changes you made to the breads that you particularly enjoyed. Every suggestion must be originally yours and we will give you credit if you want your name to appear.

The site also includes pictures of some of the finished breads and additional toppings. You may go to the web site to see if there are any exciting side dishes to compliment the bread. Like many websites, it is always in a state of change and we welcome your input and suggestions.

Question: Can the recipes in this book be used without yeast?

Answer: Yes, some of the recipes in this book may be used without yeast and we are working on others. We will intermittently be posting the results on the website. If you would like to try a recipe or two without the yeast, let us know your results and we will share it with others on the web site.

Question: What exactly does "No-Knead No-Rise" Method mean?

Answer: Since our breads are gluten--free, there is no need to knead the dough to develop the gluten. The No-Knead No-Rise Method shortens the mixing time and uses the power of the yeast in combination with the baking soda and baking powder to make the bread rise. Because time is not given for the yeast to slowly rise and make air pockets, this method often makes a denser or finer grain bread that works beautifully for many of the breads.

What is Celiac Disease or Gluten Sensitive Enteropathy?

People with celiac disease, or gluten sensitive enteropathy, cannot eat wheat, rye, or barley, in any of their forms. While celiac disease is considered uncommon by many physicians in the United States, recent studies suggest that it may be as common as 1 in every 250 Americans.

The classic presentation of celiac disease is in childhood. These youngsters usually have diarrhea, abdominal distension, and difficulty growing. However, many adults are now being diagnosed with this disorder in the United States. Adults may be found to have the disease because of gastrointestinal symptoms, or the presence of another autoimmune disease (such as Type I Diabetes, autoimmune thyroid disease and arthritis).

A particular autoimmune skin rash, called dermatitis herpetiformis, is the skin manifestation of celiac disease. It appears as red, itchy blisters on the face, trunk and extremities. Some children and adults may have no symptoms and are found through family screening or mass screenings by checking antibodies to gluten and to the intestines in a blood sample.

The gluten protein causes an immune reaction in the intestine of susceptible people. The small intestine is most affected, and prolonged damage can lead to malabsorption of sugar, protein, fat and critical vitamins and minerals. At the present time, the only known effective treatment for both celiac disease and dermatitis herpetiformis is a gluten-free diet. The minute a person begins to eat gluten-free, the intestinal healing begins, and is usually complete after six months to a year on the diet.

Being diagnosed with celiac disease early in life, and starting on a gluten-free diet, can prevent many of the complications. It has been shown in Europe that patients who were diagnosed before the age of 2 years had a much lower incidence of other autoimmune diseases later in life than those diagnosed after age 10. Adults with celiac disease who do not follow a strict gluten free diet are not only at higher risk for other types of autoimmunity, but also for small bowel lymphoma, osteoporosis and bone fractures, and chronically ill health. Patients with untreated celiac disease have two times the mortality rate of the normal population in every age group.

Blood tests can screen for celiac disease, but to confirm it a small bowel biopsy is necessary. After being gluten free for a year, a person with celiac disease can have these blood tests (antibodies) repeated, and they should be markedly improved or normal with strict adherence to the diet.

Michelle Pietzak MD
Assistant Professor of Clinical Pediatrics, University of Southern California Keck School of Medicine
Director, Center for Celiac Research-West

What is a Food Allergy?

A food allergy is an immune system response to a food that the body mistakenly believes is harmful. Once the immune system decides that a particular food is harmful, it creates specific antibodies to it.

The next time the individual eats that food, the immune system releases massive amounts of chemicals, including histamine, in order to protect the body. These chemicals trigger a cascade of allergic symptoms that can affect the respiratory system, gastrointestinal tract, skin, or cardiovascular system.

Scientists estimate that between six and seven million Americans suffer from true food allergies. At the present time, there is no cure for food allergy. Avoidance is the only way to prevent an allergic reaction.

Although an individual could be allergic to any food, such as fruits, vegetables, and meats, they are not as common as the following eight foods which account for 90 percent of all food-allergic reactions:

- Milk
- Egg
- Peanut
- Tree nut (walnut, cashew, etc.)
- Fish
- Shellfish
- Soy
- Wheat

What is the best treatment for food allergy?

Strict avoidance of the allergy-causing food is the only way to avoid a reaction. Reading ingredient labels for all foods is the key to maintaining control over the allergy. If a product doesn't have a label, allergic individuals should not eat that food. If a label contains unfamiliar terms, shoppers must call the manufacturer and ask for a definition or avoid eating that food.

Reprinted with written permission from The Food Allergy & Anaphylaxis Network (FAAN) www.foodallergy.org.

Support Groups and Reliable Sources of Information

Celiac Disease Foundation (CDF)
13251 Ventura Blvd., Suite 1
Studio City, CA 91604-1838
818.990.2354/fax 818.990.2379
www.celiac.org

Gluten Intolerance Group (GIG)
15110 10th Avenue S.W., Suite A
Seattle, WA 98166-1820
206.246.6652/fax 206.246.6531
www.gluten.net

Celiac Sprue Association (CSA/USA)
P.O. Box 31700
Omaha, NE 68131-0700
402.558.0600/fax 402.558.1347
www.csaceliacs.org

Canadian Celiac Association (CCA)
190 Britannia Road East, Unit #11
Mississauga, Ontario, Canada L4Z 1W6
905.507.6208/fax 905.507.4673
www.celiac.ca

Food Allergy & Anaphylaxis Network (FAAN)
10400 Eaton Place, Suite 107
Fairfax, VA 22030-2208
800.929.4040/fax 703.691.2713
www.foodallergy.org

Autism Research Institute
4182 Adams Avenue
San Diego, CA 92116
fax 619.563.6840
www.autism.com/ari

National Health Information Center (NHIC)
P.O. Box 1133
Washington, DC 20013-1133
800.336.4797/fax 301.984.4256
www.nhic.org

This list is just a beginning. Through these organizations you will find other reliable sources.

Resources: Gluten-Free Publications

The following is an abbreviated list of gluten-free publications. Others may be found through National Support Organizations and Information Sources.

Newsletters and Magazines

Gluten-Free Living Newsletter
A quarterly publication
P.O. Box 105
Hastings-on-Hudson, NY USA 10706
914.969.2018
E-mail: gfliving@aol.com

Living Without Magazine
A quarterly publication
P.O. Box 2126
Northbrook, IL USA 60065
847.480.8810
www.livingwithout.com

Rise 'n Shine, Gluten-Free
A quarterly newsletter for the novice and experienced GF home baker/cook
4757 E. Greenway Road, Suite, 103-#91
Phoenix, AZ 85032
Fax 602.485.4411
www.lynnrae.com

Books and Reference Material

* *Guidelines for a Gluten-Free Lifestyle*
Celiac Disease Foundation
13251 Ventura Blvd., Suite 1
Studio City, CA 91604-1838
818.990.2354
www.celiac.org

Gluten-Free Diet: A Comprehensive Resource Guide
Case Nutrition Consulting
1940 Angley Court
Regina, Saskatchewan Canada S4V 2V2
306.751.1000 phone and fax
www.glutenfreediet.ca
Shelley Case, author

* *What? No Wheat? A Lighthearted Primer to Living the Gluten-Free Wheat-Free Life*
What? No Wheat? Publishing
4757 E. Greenway Road, Suite 103-#91
Phoenix, AZ 85032
Fax 602.485.4411
www.whatnowheat.com
LynnRae Ries, author

* *Wheat-Free, Worry Free: The Art of Happy, Healthy Gluten-Free Living*
* *Kids with Celiac Disease A Family Guide to Raising Happy, Healthy, Gluten-Free Children*
Published by Hay House and Woodbine House respectively
Danna Korn, author

Cookbooks and Cooking Classes

* *Cooking Gluten-Free! A Food Lover's Collection of Chef and Family, Recipes without Gluten or Wheat*
Celiac Publishing
P.O. Box 99603
Seattle, WA 98199
206.282.4822
E-mail: celiacpublishing@earthlink.net
Karen Robertson, author

* *Delicious Gluten-Free Wheat-Free Breads: Easy to Make Breads Everyone will Love to Eat for the Bread Machine–or Oven*
What? No Wheat? Publishing
4757 E. Greenway Road, Suite 103-#91
Phoenix, AZ 85032
www.whatnowheat.com
LynnRae Ries, author

* *The Gluten-Free Gourmet Series*
Published by Henry Holt and Company
Bette Hagman, Author

Gluten-Free Baking
Published by Simon & Schuster
Rebecca Reilly, author

* *Wheat Free Recipes and Menus*
* *Special Diet Solutions*
* *Special Diet Celebrations*
Savory Palate, Inc.
8174 South Holly, Suite 404
Littleton, CO 80122-4004
800.741.5418
www.savorypalate.com
Carol Fenster, author

* *Wheat-Free, Gluten-Free Cookbook Series*
3270 Camden Rue
Cuyahoga Falls, OH 44223
330.929.1651
www.wfgf.homestead.com/gf.html
Connie Sarros, author

Glutenfreeda.com
Gluten-Free Cooking Classes in San Juan Islands
509.448.9095; 360.378.3673 fax
www.glutenfreeda.com
Jessica Hale and Yvonne Gifford

The Gluten-Free Cooking Club
Gluten-Free Cooking Classes in Phoenix, Arizona
fax 602.485.4411
www.glutenfreecookingclub.com
LynnRae Ries and Maggie Wark

Resources: Gluten-Free Baking Products

Health Food Stores and Health Food Departments of Grocery Stores are expanding their gluten-free product lines. If you do not see the items you need, ask if they will special order the item(s).

Mail Order and shopping on the Internet is a great source of gluten-free products. The following is a list of resources. Contact them for a complete listing of their gluten-free and wheat-free products. Keep in contact with the national support organizations for new resource listings.

Ancient Harvest Quinoa Corp.
222 E. Redondo Beach Blvd, Box 279
Unit B, Gardena, CA USA 90248
310.217.8125/fax 310.217.8140
www.quinoa.bigstep.com

Arrowhead Mills
Hain-Celestial Group
Box 2059
Hereford, TX 79045
800.749.0730/fax 806.364.8242

Authentic Foods
1850 W. 169th Street, Suite B
Gardena, CA 90247
800.806.4737/fax 310.366.6938
www.authenticfoods.com

Bob's Red Mill
5209 SE International Way
Milwaukee, OR 97222
800.553.2258/fax 503.653.1339
www.bobsredmill.com

'Cause You're Special!
P.O. Box 316
Phillips, WI 54555
866.669.4328/603.754.0245
www.causeyourespecial.com

El Peto Products, Ltd
41 Shoemaker St
Kitchener, ON, Canada N2E 3G9
800.387.4064/fax 519.748.5279
www.elpeto.com

Ener-G Foods, Inc.
Box 84487
Seattle, WA 98124
800.331.5222/fax 206.764.3398
www.ener-g.com

Gifts of Nature
P.O. Box 309
Corvallis, MT 59828
406.961.1529/fax 406.961.3491
www.giftsofnature.net

Gluten-Free Mall
An Internet shopping mall
Gluten-free specialty company
E-mail: info@glutenfreemall.com
www.glutenfreemall.com

Gluten Free Pantry
P.O. Box 840
Glastonbury, CT 06033
800.291.8386/fax 860.633.6853
www.glutenfreepantry.com

Gluten-Free Trading Company
604A, W. Lincoln Ave
Milwaukee, WI 53215
888.993.9933/fax 414.385.9915
www.gluten-free.net

Gluten Solutions, Inc.
An Internet grocery store
3810 Riviera Dr., Suite 1
San Diego, CA 92109
888.845.8836
www.glutensolutions.com

Minn-Dak Growers Ltd
Highway 81 North,
P.O. Box 13276
Grand Forks, ND 58208
701.746.7453/fax 701.780.9050
www.minndak.com

Miss Roben's
Box 1149
Frederick, MD 21702
800.891.0083/fax 301.665.9584
www.missroben.com

Nelson David of Canada
66 Higgins Ave
Winnipeg, MB, Canada, R3B 0A5
866.989.0379/fax 204.989.0384

New Hope Mills, Inc.
5983 Glen Haven Rd
Moravia, NY 1318
315.497.0783/fax 315.497.0810

Northern Quinoa Corp.
Box 519
Kamsack, SK, Canada, S0A 1S0
866.368.9304/306.542.3949
www.quinoa.com

Nu-World Amaranth
P.O. Box 2202
Naperville, IL 60567
630.369.6819/fax 630.369.6851
www.nuworldamaranth.com

Really Great Food Company
P.O. Box 2239
St. James, NY 11780
800.593.5377/fax 631.361.6920
www.reallygreatfood.com

Twin Valley Mills
RR #1, Box 45
Ruskin, NE 68974
402.279.3965
www.twinvalleymills.com

White Wave, Inc.
1990 N. 57th Court
Boulder, CO 80301
303.443.3470/fax 303.443.3952
www.whitewave.com

Resources: Specialty Items

The following listings are not gluten-free specific companies, but many of them carry items that may be of interest to you. .

Bickford Flavors
19007 St. Clair Avenue
Cleveland, OH 44117
800.283.8322
Gluten-free flavorings

Williams-Sonoma
Mail Order Department
P.O. Box 7456
San Francisco, CA 94120-7456
800.541.2233
www.williamssonoma.com
Vinegars, baking pans

King Arthur Flour Company
The Baker's Catalogue
P.O. Box 876
Norwich, VT 05055-0876
800.827.6836
www.kingarthurflour.com
Baking supplies

D.D. Williamson & Co., Inc.
212 Wieland Avenue
Modesto, CA 95354
TEL 1-866-412-6567 (from USA)
www.ddwilliamson.com
Caramel coloring

The Spice House
1512 North Wells Street
Chicago, IL 60610
312.274.0378
www.thespicehouse.com

Penzeys Spices
674 Grand Avenue
St. Paul, MN 55105
(651) 224-8448
www.penzeys.com

Sur La Table
P.O. Box 34707
Seattle, WA 98124
800.243.0852
www.surlatable.com
Baking supplies

The Ginger People
Royal Pacific Foods
Monterey, CA 93940
800.551.5284
www.gingerpeople.com

Your Resources:

Acknowledgments and Introductions

Delicious Gluten-Free Wheat-Free Breads was made possible through the help of these special individuals. My sincerest thanks go to:

Michelle Pietzak, M.D. for contributing to this book. A special Thanks goes to her for sharing her valuable time and contributing the important information on celiac disease and gluten intolerance to help educate and raise the awareness of others.

Mary Jo Widmer, Managing Editor, *The Food Allergy & Anaphylaxis Network* for providing permission to quote directly from their website in order to better inform those with food allergies.

Bruce Gross, Co-author, who assisted every step of the way in the development of *Delicious Gluten-Free Wheat- Free Breads*. I know he did not realize the amount of work–and fun, he was getting himself into the day he said "I'll help." Bruce approached this book, as he has done in others, in his reliable, thorough, objective, clear and concise way. His love of helping others is his form of creative baking.

Loni Frankland-Twomey, Illustrator, consistently brings joy to the projects we work on together, as well as to my life as a whole. I am thankful for her professionalism, her input, and definitely for her support in the endeavors we share. Loni's many creative abilities are expressed in her illustrations and graphic designs.

Denise Marcel, Recipe Tester and Bread Taster, challenged us to develop recipes that would respond to her "dump it all in and press Start" bread machine baking technique. This approach matches her marvelous lifestyle of simplicity and ease. Denise's skills as a warm and fuzzy dog groomer have helped her become the successful proprietor of Ma and Paws Pet Parlor in Pocatello, Idaho. Being a business woman and caring for animals is her form of creative baking.

Charlene Erpelding, Recipe Tester and Bread Taster, a diagnosed celiac and experienced baker rolled up her sleeves and jumped right in to help make *Delicious Gluten-Free Wheat-Free Breads* a success. Charlene's baking bread after bread, altering and changing recipes, sharing the breads with her family members with gluten intolerance and asking for their input, demonstrates she has an innate ability to create delicious gluten-free breads and desire to help others.

Sarah F. Day, Recipe Tester, Bread Taster, attorney and mother of a daughter diagnosed with gluten-intolerance contributed her time, her opinions, her thoughtfulness, taste tests and recipe for the Basic Sandwich Bread. Sarah's thoroughness helped us to test our recipes again and again as an added assurance other bakers would be successful using the primary baking techniques, as well as the No-Knead No-Rise Method for many of the recipes. Sarah's fabulous gluten-free baking skills make her a valuable contributor to this book.

Robert Vance, Bread Taster, offered important feedback on the bread results. He also recruited people to offer unbiased opinions on the consistency, flavor, appearance and texture of the breads. Most people did not know the breads were wheat-gluten-free and responded with favorable results.

Jeanne Basye, Recipe Tester, Bread Taster, and spouse of Jack, who must avoid gluten due to dermatitis herpetiformis, tested a significant number of recipes and taste-tested even more. Jeanne's research background helped us clarify gray areas. Her questioning mind helped everyone realize we could research, test and taste these bread recipes forever! Jeanne is a gourmet baker and loves creating recipes, cooking and baking for her husband and friends.

Tanya Chakravarty, Recipe Tester, Bread Taster and Chef, tested bread recipes in the bread machine. Tanya's keen sense of combining ingredients and accompaniments led her to contribute many of the toppings and uses for the breads in this book.

Linda Taroli, Gourmet Bread Taster pointed out breads that needed more oomph, or were wonderful as a stand alone, without any enhancements. Linda suggested toppings for a variety of breads. She tested breads in progress as well as finished recipes for an unbiased comparison. Her input on which of these breads would work best for a gluten-free lifestyle, played a valuable role in the creation of this book. She also contributed the Panettone Bread recipe that we modified to be gluten-free, and a wonderful bread.

Kathy Bowers, Bread Taster, webmaster, successfully travels camps and dines out while living the gluten-free life. Kathy tasted breads after breads while I was baking for others, as well as during the research for this book. Kathy's support of the gluten-free baking business directly contributed to the success of this book and its goal to help others.

Charlie Nygaard, Consultant, Chef, Graduate of Le Cordon Bleu, Paris, France. Charlie's chef skills and techniques were honed while traveling extensively throughout Europe and the United States, specializing as a saucier and creative chef. He owned his own restaurant and was Head Chef for Prince, the entertainer.

Elaine Monarch, Founder and Executive Director of the Celiac Disease Foundation for her support and for the wealth of information she shares, and the time she contributes to help others live a happy and healthy gluten-free life.

Cynthia Kupper, Executive Director of the Gluten Intolerance Group for her support and continual efforts to help raise awareness of gluten intolerance and improve the life of others.

My special thanks go to Vern, my life partner for almost 25 years. When I first started baking, he always sampled what I baked, no matter how it looked. He agreed to a gluten-free kitchen. He attended conferences and gluten-free cooking and baking classes with me so I could get "a handle" on what it meant to be gluten-free and learn how to bake from the specialists.

As my baking skills increased and other gluten-free people started purchasing home made breads, rolls, cookies and desserts from me, Vern would wait patiently, or make dinner himself, while I baked to fill gluten-free orders instead of making dinner. While working on this book, he lived with our kitchen filled with every flour imaginable and seven bread machines on the counters. On extremely busy days, he simply rolled his eyes when my reply to "What's for dinner?" was..."Bread". Finally, after about the 300th loaf of bread that I made, he starting asking, "Are you making dinner recipes in your next cookbook?"

An important thanks goes to over 50 Bread Tasters from different areas of the country and different walks of life. Some of the Bread Tasters are on gluten-free diets and some are not.

Susan Summers
Russ Boocock
Sheila Boocock
Maurice Arieli
Ruth Arieli
Kathy Bowers
Linda Taroli
Jessica Tapia
Jan Vidimos
Gaye Lloyd
Delores Butler
Jeanne Basye
Jack Basye
Tanya Chakravarty
Sarah Day
Hannah Day
Barbara Hicks
Maggie Wark
Vern Lang
Robert Lang
Gerri Lang
Denise Marcel
Doug Magee
Dora Guidotti
Donna Moser
Jack Stoltz
Vicki Bizallion
Tess Verderber
Tess Magee
Katy Patrick
Bruce Gross
Jean Michaelski
Sherry Nighswonger
Bea Sims
Linda Collins
Gayle Mara
Debbie Perales
Michael Allen
Michael Allen's Family
LaDonna Hoyt
LaDonna Hoyt's Family
Jim Ramos
Fran Thompson
Simon Tringstrom
Cecilia Lopez
Judy Tobia
Sofia Eneqvist,
Sofia's Mom and Dad
Ida Swahn
Raquel Seminario
Charlene Erpelding
Cory Erpelding
Brian Erpelding
Robert Vance
Shanna Murphree
Lucille Hickson
Gloria Palumbo
Denise Taylor
Yvonne and Alma
Moreno

Mindy Collier for contribution of Dill and Cottage Cheese Bread, a family recipe that we converted to gluten-free.

To all these people, and more, Thank You.

Meet the Testers and Learn Their Techniques

Denise Marcel, Recipe Tester, Bread Taster, Coordinator

LynnRae did not realize, when she requested I test recipes, what a unique Tester I am.

I am not much of a cook or baker and therein lay my strength as a Tester. It is important to note that for all my lack of expertise, all my incorrect measuring, substituting, and other misunderstandings, all the recipes produced loaves of delectable bread.

I am a highly trained dog groomer and owner of Ma and Paws Pet Parlor in Idaho. The owners of two of my good customers have either wheat allergies or are gluten intolerant.

Busy is my middle name. I am dedicated to my "pawed" clientele. I quilt, do needlework and am in the middle of writing a book on how to groom the home pet. So I do not have time for elaborate meals, fancy social activities or baking bread from scratch.

That is where the beauty of the bread machine came in.

I used the basic method. I never pre-mixed anything. I put all the liquid ingredients directly into the bread pan, and then I measured all the dry ingredients directly into the pan. I selected the Basic Cycle and hit the Start button. Then I walked away. I liked this method. Hint: I would suggest to bakers that they try to break their egg yolks over the paddle of the bread maker. Not only is this fun but also it ensures that the paddle is in the bread maker.

I rarely helped the bread machine mix the ingredients within the first 10 minutes. The worst that happened was that a couple of the bread loaf corners were white from unmixed flour. But that did not bother us.

From time to time I had to add more water to the ingredients when the machine was mixing. I could tell because the bread machine would start jumping around or gave a slow whirring noise.

Usually I would bring bread to the "shop" for little tasting parties. Everyone loved the breads and people asked for the recipes, even though they did not need to be "wheat-free".

My breads from the recipes in this book were successful from the very beginning. I substituted flours on some of the recipes because some of the products were not available in my town. And the breads still came out delicious.

I baked each of the breads I made in two different ways—the One Step Method and the No-Knead No-Rise Method. I liked the speed of the No-Knead No-Rise Method, but I liked the texture, flavor and crumb of the One Step, Basic Cycle Method the most.

So my suggestion to you is to relax, pick a recipe, put the ingredients in and push the Start button. You are in for a treat.

Charlene Erpelding, Recipe Tester, Bread Taster and Recipe Creator

Growing up and living on a farm in Iowa, I learned from childhood on that we were self-sufficient. My Mother, like many mothers, did lots of cooking and baking. Of course, there was always a large garden so we could can and freeze the extra fruits and vegetables for the winter months. We also raised live stock and chickens, so we had fresh eggs and meat. We had a milk cow, so thanks to Dad, always had fresh milk, cream and made our own butter and cottage cheese.

I enjoyed baking and cooking and considered myself pretty good at baking breads, cakes, cookies and pies, and of course, making meals. Nothing ever failed! I was a 4H leader and learned from the county home economist about food storage, nutrition and also preparing and serving meals.

After being diagnosed with celiac, and trying my baking skills with the "new gluten-free" flours, all that came to an end. It seemed like nothing would turn out right. I threw away lots of failures. Getting discouraged, I gave up on baking for a time.

After talking to others, I began to learn how to bake with the gluten-free flours. Plus, testing and creating recipes for *Delicious Gluten-Free Wheat-Free Breads* with LynnRae helped restore my bread baking confidence. I have learned the versatilities of the bread machine with combining the various flours allowed for those who have celiac disease or gluten intolerance.

By using these recipes, I have found that I can substitute starches and many of the flours in one-half cup increments. That doesn't mean that I don't have a flop from time to time. Baking is a challenge because of the large number of variables, but with this book there are many possible variations to recipes that make it easier. Experimenting with these bread recipes was very gratifying and enjoyable.

Here are some of the techniques I used when baking these recipes: I am a "dipper. When I was growing up, Mother always bought flour in big 25 lb. cloth flour sacks. I grew up dipping into the sack to measure the flour and sugar, and I still do. I usually make sure all ingredients are room temperature. I mix all the liquids together, and then I mix all the dry ingredients together in a separate bowl. First I pour the liquid mixture into the bread pan and then the dry mixture. I put the raisins, fruit, and nuts in from the beginning, instead of waiting for the "beep" on the bread machine. I find that by adding the nuts, raisins and fruits in the beginning, they seem to be distributed more evenly in the finished product. I do, however, wait when adding chocolate chips.

I prefer the Two-Step Method. I think the breads seem to be a little moister than when they go through the whole cycle, even though some of the breads come out the same.

I also like the No-Knead No-Rise Method for some of the breads, particularly the pumpernickel.

The breads with more extra ingredients, such as nuts and fruits and vegetables, seem to be heavier and more dense when using the No-Knead No-Rise Method.

It has been interesting having the family taste these breads. Two of my four sons are also celiac. The grandchildren also helped to taste the breads. They really like the Lemon Poppy Seed.

My youngest son, Cory has Dermatitis Herpetiformis. He loves the Rye Bread with Sauerkraut. He found out that it is also his cat Oliver's favorite. My oldest son loves tasting these breads, even though he doesn't have celiac.

Brian also has Dermatitis Herpetiformis. He enjoyed the Pizza Bread and said it even smelled like the real thing. A niece came over one Saturday when I was baking and wanted to know if this bread would hurt her, because she wanted to taste them. She said she could not tell that they didn't have wheat flour in them and said they were very good.

Testing and baking these breads has been fun and interesting. Even some of the flops have been an "eye opener".

Some of the toppings that the family likes are whipped topping on the Date Nut Bread and Chocolate Cherry Breads; Flavored strawberry cream cheese on the Strawberry-Banana Bread; lemon cream cheese on the Lemon Poppy Seed Bread; and peanut butter and honey on the Peanut and Uncola Bread. The Apricot Bread is delicious with Apricot Preserves. Apple butter on the Apple bread is perfect for breakfast.

Some observations: Do not combine dates and sorghum flour; we did not like how they tasted together. The same is true for the combination of pumpkin and quinoa flour.

Bruce Gross, Co-Author, Recipe Tester, Bread Taster, and Coordinator

I wanted to buy a bread machine for many years. I am a good cook, but I have never been a baker, so I was uncertain about where to start.

Helping people is my profession. I am a Human Resource Generalist in the San Francisco Bay Area, and before that I was a customer service representative.

So when LynnRae told me she was creating recipes for gluten-free, wheat-free breads, I immediately asked if I could roll up my sleeves and assist.

I had worked with LynnRae in the Beauty and Art Industries a couple of years ago, writing educational manuals and producing training videos, so this was right up my alley.

In addition, this was perfect since I had recently met people in my neighborhood who were gluten-intolerant. They were equally as enthused about this new bread book project.

The next thing I knew, I was shopping for bread machines and new flours. Of course, just about any flour was new to me, but sorghum, teff, amaranth, rice flour and xanthan gum were totally foreign words.

I purchased a moderately priced bread machine and found three health food-type stores where I could purchase the needed flours. One of our goals for the book *Delicious Gluten-Free Wheat-Free Breads* was that expensive equipment was not needed in order to bake the recipes. So I also purchased a garage sale bread machine for recipe testing.

For the next eight months my profession by day was Human Resource Generalist and at night I transformed into bread machine Tester, recipe scrutinizer and bread Taster. At one time I had three bread machines operating in my kitchen. Every day I would bring new breads into work that I had baked from the recipes in this book and received feedback from a dozen people. Everyone enjoyed tasting the breads, giving feedback and taking their favorite breads home, even though they did not have to eat gluten-free.

As I started baking, I learned that it pays to follow the recipe instructions the first time. I seldom had any flops when testing and re-testing the recipes in *Delicious Gluten-Free Wheat-Free Breads*. And when I did, it usually was because I didn't remember if I had put in that last cup of flour, or the yeast, or the add-ins.

I was meticulous in the beginning. I made sure the eggs and the egg whites all equaled ¾ cup, and measured each and every liquid ingredient to the exact amount. I measured and then re-measured the flour mixture. I went specifically by each instruction and worried about whether I should "plump" the raisins before I added them or if I should just put them in dry.

By the time I made the same recipe twice, I was able to relax and not worry about measuring to the smallest detail, or some of the other particulars. As time went on, I started experimenting with using egg whites or egg replacer instead of using eggs.

Each time I tried something new, it was exciting to find the substitutes were successful and I had great looking and tasting loaves of bread!

As I became more comfortable with the gluten-free/wheat-free breads and the different mixing and baking techniques, LynnRae asked if I would like to create some recipes to contribute to the book. She didn't need to ask a second time. I am certain you will find the same desire to be creative and make different breads from these recipes. That is why we have included a form for you to "personalize" the bread to your particular taste and style.

I baked every recipe at least three different ways. In my opinion, each method worked and can be used for specific purposes. These are my suggestions:

- The One-Step Method is ideal for when there is a multitude of things going on and no time to pay attention to the bread, except for the first 10 minutes when I watch the dough to determine if it needs more water or extra ingredients.
- The Two-Step Method is perfect for when I want to be "pickier" about how my bread turns out.
- The No-Knead No-Rise method is best for when I am behind schedule. It is one of my favorite methods.
- The oven method caters to my need to make rolls, or other baked goods.

I found making and creating the recipes to be a great hobby. It was a wonderful way to interact with my family and friends—and I was able to enjoy some of the most delicious breads I have ever tasted.

I trust you will enjoy the bread recipes and information as much as we enjoyed creating them for you and your family.

About the Author

LynnRae Ries graduated Magna Cum Laude from the University of Minnesota with a degree in Business and Communication; was referenced in *Who's Who of American Women* and has created a number of successful start up businesses. She has authored and published "how-to" books and videos in the beauty and art industries. As owner of SFN Art Co., she traveled extensively presenting marketing seminars and how-to classes.

LynnRae was diagnosed with celiac disease in October of 1999. For almost three years she assisted a local support group in their start up and growth by serving on the board, chairing special functions and contributing as co-webmaster. She has conducted restaurant reviews, developed gluten-free-friendly menus, and assisted in raising awareness to gluten-free dining. For three years LynnRae operated a personal baking service that specializes in gluten-free breads, cookies and desserts.

LynnRae resides in Arizona with Vern and their four dogs, Duffy, Jackie, Smokie and Angelo. She studies gourmet cooking at various schools, interviews restaurants and publishes *Gluten-Free e-News,* a free on-line newsletter for the celiac community. Her first book, *What? No Wheat? A Lighthearted Primer to Living the Gluten-Free Wheat-Free Life,* is endorsed by Doctors and Executive Directors of National Support Organizations.

When LynnRae is not researching or writing a new book, attending classes or volunteering at national celiac and gluten intolerance conferences, you will find her teaching Gluten-Free Cooking classes at the *Gluten-Free Cooking Club.* She is founder of The Gluten-Free Group, an on-line support group that meets in Arizona, www.glutenfreegroup.com; and author of *Rise and Shine, Gluten-Free,* a quarterly newsletter written for both the novice and the experienced home baker/chef. Visit her web page at www.lynnrae.com.

About the Illustrator

Loni Frankland-Twomey is an Ohioan, who has made her home and business in the San Francisco Bay Area since 1980. Always interested in art, she pursued commercial art in high school and college, graduating from the Art Institute of Pittsburgh, Pennsylvania in Visual Communications. After graduation she designed for ad agencies and printers in Philadelphia, then started her own successful company, Arts Unlimited, in Livermore, California. Loni is a fine art painter, using oils, acrylics, watercolors, and airbrush in her illustrations, murals and cartoons. She is presently working on a video production.

LynnRae and Loni have worked together since 1988 and have become the best of friends.

Index

Also from What? No Wheat? Publishing

What? No Wheat?
A Lighthearted Primer to Living the Gluten-Free Wheat-Free Life

By LynnRae Ries

"LynnRae Ries, with the illustration help of her business associate and friend, Loni Frankland-Twomey, has provided a great service to the gluten-free and celiac communities with LynnRae's lighthearted book, *What? No Wheat?*

Based on her personal experiences, and those of many others, LynnRae takes us though all the stages of having to deal with a gluten-free lifestyle: from medical diagnosis, mourning the loss of favorite foods, and the trial of baking—to the challenges of eating out, dealing with family and friends, and taking on the rest of the world.

LynnRae certainly knows how to make lemonade out of lemons.

I am sure that everyone who reads this book will either see themselves, or someone they know, depicted in these all too true situations! And hopefully, they will ultimately reach the same conclusions as 'Gloria' and 'Jason,' the characters in this book—that 'gluten-free' can be a wonderful life."

From Foreword by Michelle Pietzak, M.D., Director

Endorsed by Michelle Pietzak, M.D., Director, Center for Celiac Research, West
Elaine Monarch, Founder/Executive Director, CDF
Cynthia Kupper, R.D. C.D., Executive Director, GIG
Cynthia Rudert, M.D., Medical Advisor to CDF and GIG
Peter H.R. Green, M.D., Director, Celiac Disease Center at Columbia University

$9.95 paper ISBN 0-9724154-0-8 8"x8"
90 pages includes 29 cartoon illustrations www.whatnowheat.com

If a gluten-free or wheat-free lifestyle is for you...

Then you will love *Rise and Shine, Gluten-Free*, a quarterly newsletter written for both the novice and the experienced gluten-free or wheat-free home baker/chef.

Some of the topics covered throughout the year may include:

- readers questions and answers
- how to be creative with gluten-free mixes
- casein free recipes and special diet substitutions
- recipes for baking other "goodies" in your bread machine
- tips on flours and other gluten-free/wheat-free ingredients
- bread machine features and how to make the best purchase
- tested, tasted and tested-again recipes for the bread machine
- hints on shopping for verifiable gluten-free wheat-free items
- contests and opportunities for readers to submit their own recipes
- recipes for creating breads in the oven, and different types of ovens
- recipes and hints for creating delicious and wonderful cookies, brownies, pizzas, cakes, pies, biscotti, appetizers, stuffing and more

---

Annual subscriptions are only $18.00 in the USA, plus $6.95 mailing and handling.

To start your subscription, send a check in United States funds, made payable to **What? No Wheat?**

What? No Wheat?
4757 East Greenway Road Suite 103-#91
Phoenix, Az 85032

Or visit our website at www.whatnowheat.com or www.LynnRae.com
Please make certain your full name, mailing address and zip code are included and easy to read. Include a phone number or e-mail address should we need to reach you.

Order Form

Fax orders: 602.485.4411. Send this form.
Telephone orders: Call 602.485.8751. Have your credit card ready.
E-mail orders: whatnowheat@whatnowheat.com
Orders by mail:: What? No Wheat?, 4757 E. Greenway Rd. Suite 103-#91
Phoenix, AZ 85032-8510

Please send the following books and newsletter subscriptions:

	Qty**	Price	Total
What? No Wheat?		$ 9.95	
Delicious Gluten-Free Breads		$16.95	
Rise and Shine, Gluten-Free A Quarterly baking/cooking newsletter		$24.95	
Sales tax: Add 7.5% for books shipped to Arizona address.			
U.S. Shipping, add $4.00 for first book/$2.00 for each additional book. *			
Total enclosed or to be charged on credit card			

*Fax address for shipping quote outside of U.S. **Quantity discounts available**

Payment Type (check one): ❑ Money Order ❑ Check ❑ Credit card

Ship To:

Name:____
Address:______________________________________
City:____________________State:______Zip:__________
Telephone:________________E-mail address:______________

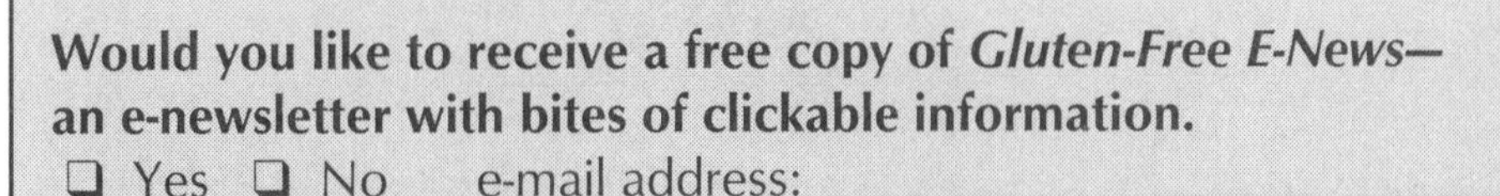

Would you like to receive a free copy of *Gluten-Free E-News*— an e-newsletter with bites of clickable information.
❑ Yes ❑ No e-mail address:________________________

Please check one: ❑ Visa ❑ MasterCard

Card number:____
Name on card:________________________Exp. date:____________

Provide credit card billing address if it is different than the ship to address:

Billing Address:____________________________________
City:____________________State:______Zip:__________
Billing Phone No.:________________________

Letter from a Bread Recipe Tester

Hi!

Celiac disease runs in my father's side of the family. I have been on a gluten-free "lifestyle" vs "diet" for a couple of years.

After trying to use various recipes, some of which were "interesting" to say the least, I was hesitant to be part of a "tasting group" for gluten-free breads.

That apprehension vanished immediately upon tasting the first slice of bread. In fact, I have felt "as rich as a king," as some days I came home with up to 10 different kinds of breads!

As I savored each slice, tasting and commenting, it was hard to believe that these breads actually were gluten-free.

This book is going to be a blessing to all who use it—children will love the Pizza, Chicken and Peppers, and the Caribbean Sweet Bread, to name a few. Adults will enjoy the vast varieties that are available for all occasions.

The recipes are specially written for bread machines and are as "no fail" as possible and have been repeatedly tested and tasted.

As someone who thought that they were limited to "Rice Bread" the rest of their life, I wholeheartedly endorse this wonderful cookbook that provides specialty bread recipes in an easy to follow format.

Gaye Lloyd